PURE Luxury

WORLD'S BEST HOUSES

PURE *Luxury*

WORLD'S BEST HOUSES

Edited by Driss Fatih

images
Publishing

Published in Australia in 2012 by
The Images Publishing Group Pty Ltd
ABN 89 059 734 431
6 Bastow Place, Mulgrave, Victoria 3170, Australia
Tel: +61 3 9561 5544 Fax: +61 3 9561 4860
books@imagespublishing.com
www.imagespublishing.com

Copyright © The Images Publishing Group Pty Ltd 2012
The Images Publishing Group Reference Number: 1029

National Library of Australia Cataloguing-in-Publication entry:

Author: Fatih, Driss
Title: Pure luxury: world's best houses / Driss Fatih.
ISBN: 9781864704969 (hbk)
Subjects: Architecture, Modern – Pictorial works.
                 Architecture, Domestic – Pictorial works.
Dewey Number: 728

Edited by Driss Fatih

Designed by The Graphic Image Studio Pty Ltd, Mulgrave, Australia
www.tgis.com.au

Pre-publishing services by United Graphic Pte Ltd, Singapore
Printed by 1010 Printing International Limited in China
on 140 gsm Gold East Matt Art paper

IMAGES has included on its website a page for special
notices in relation to this and our other publications.
Please visit www.imagespublishing.com

Contents

Contents _continued_

luxury | ˈlək sh (ə)rē |

<u>noun</u> (pl. **-ries**)
the state of great comfort and extravagant
living: *he lived a life of luxury.*

<u>adjective</u>
luxurious or of the nature of a luxury:
a luxury house | luxury goods.

Introduction

Luxury is the pinnacle of civilized living: it brings to mind a state of refinement, of comfort, and of sensuous pleasure. It evokes abundance, and can be interpreted in any number of ways, but it is always desirable. And desirable, irrespective of location – be it the glamorous Hollywood Hills, the rugged terrain of the South Island of New Zealand, the lush green forests of the Baltics, or the tropical setting of Singapore or Jakarta.

The projects in this book are the embodiment of luxury – they offer their owners a home, a place of private refuge from a world which never stops turning; an uncertain world where few things can be taken for granted as they were in the past. But these houses are more than just homes and offer more than just a place to eat, unwind and sleep.

Some of these houses are at the cutting edge of the modern – minimalist geometric designs of glass, steel and clean lines offer transparency and simplicity in an ever-busier and complicated world: the luxury of rising above the throng and leaving the rat-race behind. Others offer the inhabitants a rural idyll – a place for affluent city dwellers to luxuriate in the grandeur and calm of nature.

While others allow the owners to employ the very latest in computer technology to regulate how they live – whether communications, entertainment, heating or cooling the space they inhabit or even incorporating fully-operating studios or offices at home.

This is the luxury of choice, above all – the highest aspiration in today's consumer society.

Luxury is in the eye of the beholder, as these houses testify. Some might appear monolithic at first – brutally minimalistic, even; but through clever use of sliding doors, split levels, breezeways and often simply the changing light of day, they allow private spaces to become public, or vice versa, allowing different generations of the same family to live in harmony – true luxury indeed.

Other houses are more subtle, and work in harmony with their natural environment. Some of them become a part of the environment quite literally, built into the lie of the land – be it a cliff face, a hill, or a beachside – and harness local, renewable materials. The luxury of being at one with nature and saving the planet at the same time.

Living in the heart of a metropolis in an unrelenting climate of heat, humidity, pollution and hustle and bustle hardly conjures up luxury, to most people; yet several houses within these pages pull off luxury living, combining authentic Asian interiors – hosting family members from across the generations – with all mod-cons. Some feature interior gardens integrated into the house itself, a green sanctuary allowing the inhabitants to breathe pure, clean air – a precious luxury in the Big Smoke.

I hope you will enjoy leafing through the pages of this lovingly compiled book, and indulge yourself for a few minutes in the sheer quality and range of modern residential architecture on show.

Driss Fatih
Editor

***** (Five Star) House

Carol Kurth Architecture, PC
Westchester, New York, USA

On a bucolic tree-lined street that was once farmland, set back from the road, an old dilapidated house was demolished to make way for a new home. The site, though lush and level, was challenging with respect to the size and complexity of the client's programme and its context within an established neighbourhood. Wetlands restrictions and tree ordinances as well as constraints of lot width and setback requirements added further to the issues that needed to be addressed.

In response to the site constraints, the new home is designed as an assemblage of buildings, articulated yet connected to one another architecturally. The different volumes express the functionality of the elements within. A unifying barn-style structure contains the main living spaces of the home, while adjunct structures contain the elements of a 'hotel at home', hence the 'five star' designation. These amenities – an indoor pool/spa area, indoor basketball/sports court, exercise area, guest suite and separate stone building for additional garage space – reflect the owners' lifestyle and passion for wellness, health and tranquility for themselves and their family.

Natural materials such as indigenous fieldstone, barn siding and cedar shakes, implemented in a manner to enhance the identity of each structure, advance the concept of a village of buildings as part of the whole. The house is linked together by a two-storey stone wall that is expressed on the interior and exterior to create an interplay between the inside and outside. The landscape echoes the concept and is created as an 'exterior room' defined by trees and plantings.

The interiors were designed to embody a serene minimalist aesthetic throughout. The architect, client and interior design firm MA-DS worked in tandem to accomplish the textured backdrop. An interior gallery-style axis along the expressed stone wall serves as a circulation spine, creating the flow of spaces within. Cupolas and expressed stair elements, reminiscent of barns, add illumination to the interiors. The gym structure, partially recessed underground, benefits from added illumination via clerestory windows. A retractable roof and series of glass doors along with a flow of materials from interior to exterior add to the feeling of an indoor–outdoor environment at the pool area. ***** (Five Star) House is a spacious family retreat that embraces the conventional vernacular of the neighbourhood, the property's farmstead history and the clients' modern aesthetic.

Photography: Peter Krupenye

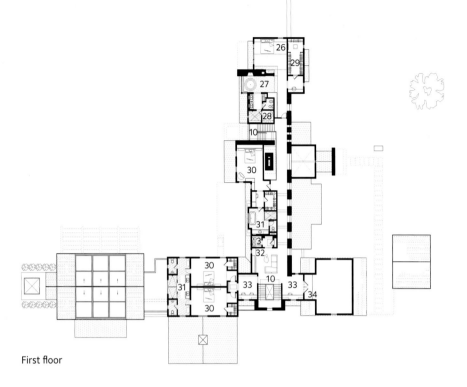

First floor

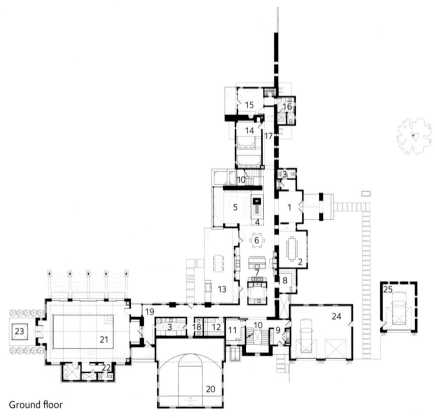

Ground floor

1 Entry foyer
2 Dining room
3 Powder room
4 Fireplace
5 Living room
6 Breakfast room
7 Kitchen
8 Study
9 Mud room
10 Stairwell
11 Study
12 Service area
13 Patio/barbecue
14 Theatre/lounge
15 Guest bedroom
16 Guest ensuite
17 Gallery
18 Pantry
19 Laundry
20 Gym (below)
21 Indoor pool
22 Pool bathroom
23 Outdoor hot tub
24 Two-car garage
25 Single-car garage
26 Master bedroom
27 Master ensuite
28 Sauna
29 Walk-in wardrobe
30 Bedroom
31 Ensuite
32 Children's lounge
33 Homework area
34 Store

0   5m

4430 Abbott Avenue

Morrison Dilworth + Walls
Dallas, Texas, USA

This home occupies a site in one of the more interesting neighbourhoods of Dallas, in terms of residential architecture. Originally the neighbourhood consisted of small bungalows on lots of 700 square metres (7,500 square feet). Over the last 30 years development of the neighbourhood has consisted of modern, high-end townhouses and several single-family homes. This house represents the latest addition to that neighbourhood.

The home itself was designed for a single man who entertains frequently and is building an art collection. The house proper occupies the northern half of the site to maximise the space available for a courtyard and pool. The main living spaces and kitchen open directly onto the courtyard. A teak screen was employed in the front of the house to provide scale, texture and shading, as well as to diffuse views into the house from passing traffic, both pedestrian and vehicular.

Photography: Charles Smith

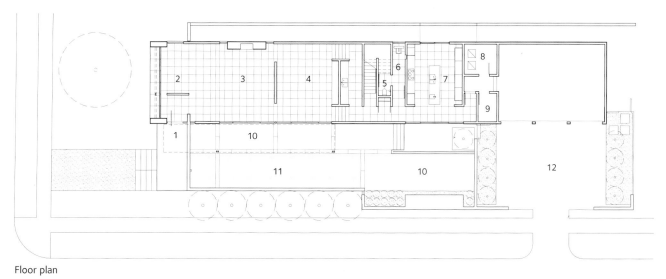

1 Entry
2 Dining area
3 Living area
4 Media room
5 Powder room
6 Pantry
7 Kitchen
8 Laundry
9 Store
10 Terrace
11 Pool
12 Motor court

Floor plan

0   4m

The Architect's Residence

Carlos Bratke Architect
São Paulo, Brazil

The central idea of this design is a large metallic covering that works as an envelope wrapping around a conventional house. The lot where the house is situated is 4 metres lower than the street level, which suggested an inversion of the traditional two-storey townhouse. Therefore the main access to the house is at street level through the living room, while the bedrooms are downstairs in the space created by the difference in level.

This inversion allowed the creation of a huge void some 16 metres by 16 metres square over the floor of the ground-level rooms, at street level; this would be a structural problem if applied to the traditional townhouse, where the bedrooms are upstairs. With this metallic trussed-beam structure it was possible to attain a huge open space – the living room, and most important part of the house.

The most complicated part of the construction of this roof-top structure was not the trussed-beam void, but the solution adopted to span the perpendicular line from the ridge beam to the pillar. The final decision rested on a structure comprising two metallic sheets 15 centimetres apart with Styrofoam plates between them. Inside these plates 50 spars were forced in the opposite direction by a jack and riveted and supported on a thin concrete pillar. This process ended up creating a pre-stressed structure working under tensile stress on its lower part, and compression stress on its upper part.

Beside its unique and technologically innovative shape, the roof-top has also contributed to the acoustic comfort of the house, located on a very noisy avenue in the Morumbi district of São Paulo.

Photography: Cacá Bratke, José Moscardi, Jr

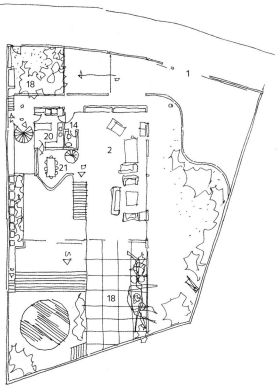

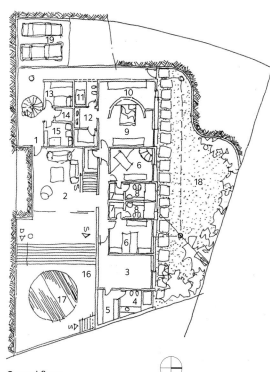

Lower ground floor

Ground floor

1 Entry
2 Living room
3 TV room
4 Bathroom
5 Closet
6 Bedroom
7 Walk-in wardrobe
8 Ensuite
9 Master bedroom
10 Master walk-in wardrobe
11 Master ensuite
12 Master water closet
13 Utility room
14 Water closet
15 Laundry
16 Deck
17 Pool
18 Garden
19 Garage
20 Kitchen
21 Dining room

17

BC House Gilberto L. Rodríguez

GLR Arquitectos
Monterrey, Mexico

BC House sits in a privileged topographical spot, overlooking houses in the surrounding area. The owners enjoy excellent views towards Chipinque National Park to the south, as well as towards the east, which is dominated on the horizon by the Cerro de la Silla, an emblematic hill on the edge of the city of Monterrey. Access to the site is on the north side, ascending through a long slope that leads to the highest level, where the floor plan is located. With simple, pure geometric volumes, concealing rather challenging structural solutions, the project evokes an image of lightness within a language of heavy and massive volumes.

Although colour does not have a major presence in the architect's work, this project takes an important step forward into the exploration of new materials – black granite and white exposed concrete create a stark impression, together with the striking effect the exposed steel elements lend to the building. Beyond its bio-climatic function, the implementation of green roofs as a way to integrate the landscape serves to preserve the natural appearance of the environment, dominated by the presence of the breathtaking Sierra Madre mountain range.

The house was conceived as a sustainable house from the beginning and is highly energy-efficient. The architect studied the sun's trajectory and the prevailing winds through the different seasons of the year and as a result, the house has diverse systems of isolation, such as double-thickness walls filled with polyisocyanurate, an ecologically-sound thermal insulator; double-glazed windows with low emissivity (Low-E) glass; systems of pluvial water-harvesting and grey water treatment for irrigation; solar paddles for pool-heating and garden-illumination; solar water-heaters; hydronic heating systems to reduce power consumption; south-facing skylights; and a landscape project featuring native vegetation.

Photography: Jorge Taboada

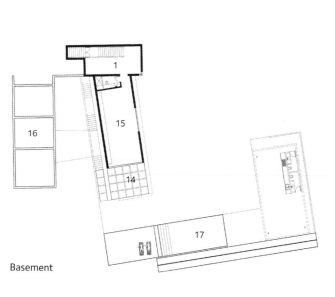

Basement

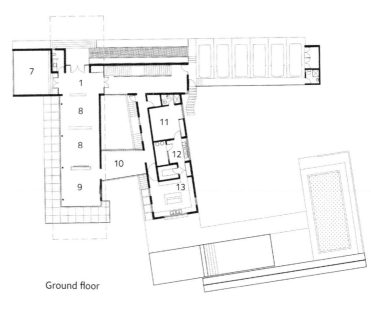

Ground floor

1 Foyer
2 Bedroom
3 Master bedroom
4 Dressing room
5 Internal patio
6 Machine room
7 Library
8 Living room
9 Dining room
10 Connecting room
11 Service room
12 Laundry room
13 Kitchen
14 Covered terrace
15 Games room
16 Garage
17 Pool

0   5m

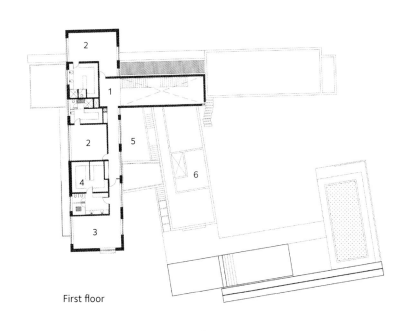

First floor

Beach Front Property

Mitchell Freedland Design
West Vancouver, British Columbia, Canada

This 116-square-metre (1250 square feet) construction project constituted the addition of a master suite to an existing modernist beach house by Nick Milkovich and Arthur Erickson, located on a steep site with spectacular vistas. The design challenge was to create a seamless interior envelope that complements the minimal outer structure, while infusing a sense of warmth and originality to the new environment. The floor plan was a direct response to the panoramic views and the building's trapezoidal footprint; naturally, the lounge and bedroom were to engage the view.

The design task deepened with the interior designer's suggestion that the bath and vanity area share this spectacular advantage point. A feature element of media and fire was positioned as an organisational device between the lounge and bed, while a Starphire glass partition served to define the bed and bath areas. This careful placement affords paramount views from the bathing area. Skylights were introduced to announce the bath area and provide more natural light. The form and rhythm of these follow the existing skylights in the lower floor, bowing to the established vocabulary. The ceiling was dropped over the open bath and wood-panelled rear plane, to reinforce the nexus point where these two elements intersect. The edge of this drop was lit to highlight the ceiling form and celebrate the window-height of the primary area.

The material palette was purposefully minimal so as not to compete with the extraordinary views. The inclusion of rift-cut white oak panelling successfully grounds the rear of the suite from the view and brings the sense of warmth the client desired. One exception to this controlled scheme is the taupe velvet draped closet, acting as a sensuous counterpoint to the restrained suite – a surprise element that the client loved. The warmth, comfort and elegance (instilled into this pure aesthetic) made it an original and fresh addition to the minimalist beach house, exceeding the client's expectations and vision.

Photography: Ed White

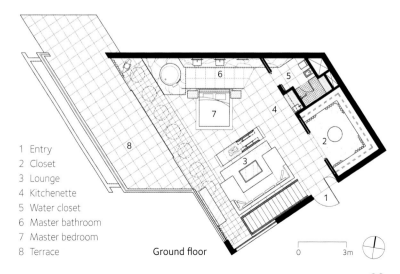

1 Entry
2 Closet
3 Lounge
4 Kitchenette
5 Water closet
6 Master bathroom
7 Master bedroom
8 Terrace

Ground floor

0   3m

Blomfield Spa | Architektur Ltd
Takapuna Beach, Auckland, New Zealand

The owners of this property had already been living in an old two-storey house on this site, so had very particular requirements for certain spaces relative to views and orientations, which were well thought out. This made designing the house a pleasure, as designer and client shared an understanding of the circumstances.

The slope of the site and the location of a large protected pohutukawa tree (which dominates the street-side of the property) meant that basement garaging was the obvious solution.

The clients wanted some separation from their teenage children, so the first floor became a master suite, including bedroom, walk-in wardrobe, ensuite, lounge and his and hers studies. The children's bedrooms are on the ground floor, on the same level as the main living areas, kitchen and outside decks around the pool.

Some of the most striking features of the exterior of the house are the louvers – horizontal, elliptical aluminium blades on the street side, with softer, vertical cedar-timber fins on the north-west elevation. These have been designed to allow shading at particular times of day and year and create privacy as well as interest to the façades.

A sand-coloured blockwork base grounds the house, while the cedar-clad top storey hovers above, offering both sheltered outdoor living below and a contrast of materiality. The colour palate is in keeping with its beachside location, just two houses back from Takapuna Beach.

Photography: James Blackwood

Ground floor

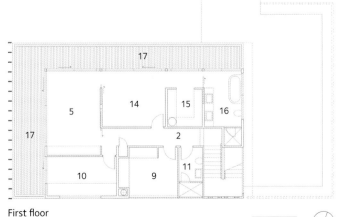

First floor

1 Entry from basement
2 Hall
3 Dining room
4 Living room
5 Lounge
6 Kitchen
7 Pantry
8 Laundry
9 Bedroom
10 Study
11 Bathroom
12 Gym/rumpus room
13 Water closet
14 Master bedroom
15 Walk-in wardrobe
16 Ensuite
17 Deck

0   3m

Brighton House

Robert Simeoni Architects
Brighton, Victoria, Australia

The architect's brief was to create a light-filled family house that makes the most of the site. The 965-square-metre (10,400 square feet) plot is nearly flat, on a street of already substantial suburban blocks. It was noted that the character of this suburb is rapidly changing from the dominant old model of the villa with a front and back yard, to a new model of the villa with little front yard. In this sense the house is conservative: a tall, mature tree on the street front suggests a return to the old model. But while most traditional houses in the street are demonstrative about their presence, this house's wide front is broken into three and the mass is dispersed; coloured with neutral shades of zinc and concrete, it defers to the principal streetscape furniture: namely, the tree.

The block guided the design towards other results too, its width making possible a house largely enclosed from the side boundaries, where planning regulations discourage overlooking. It instead opens onto a central north-facing courtyard. This courtyard was conceived as an empty space to look through or down into rather than to occupy – a canopy hovering above, ambiguously enclosing it in part, creating a kind of shelter. Halfway between courtyard and backyard there is a place for the family to gather for meals in the fresh air, where they can view the clear, bright sun from the cool, deep shade.

Contradictory terms of scale are negotiated to redress intimacy in an otherwise expansive programme. The building encourages an ambiguity of appearance as both singular object and multiple entity – between the singularity of the room and open space. The circuitous nature of moving through it and around it aims for a fluctuation between the two states. Spatial overlap is repeated as a design strategy so that the relationship between room and passage becomes at points deliberately unclear.

Light is directed through and across spaces and bounces off surfaces – an awareness of the building's orientation used to create a variety of different natural lighting conditions appropriate to the use of each room. The parents' study is an introspective room with no long view out. It has four differently oriented natural light sources, its character shifting throughout the day, but always lit diffusely for reading.

Throughout the home and across scales, asymmetry is favoured. There is a cultivated sense of the incomplete, arising from the invention of a pre-existing condition – an archeological-like set of structures made of pre-cast and *in situ* concrete that are in turns built over, around and strategically revealed.

Photography: John Gollings and Trevor Mein

Ground floor

First floor

1	Entry	12	Lounge
2	Den	13	Library
3	Kitchen	14	Void
4	Dining area	15	Guest bedroom
5	Living area	16	Ensuite
6	Open courtyard	17	Bedroom
7	Outdoor dining area	18	Study
8	Children's room	19	Bathroom
9	Laundry	20	Master bedroom
10	Powder room	21	Master ensuite
11	Dining room	22	Walk-in wardrobe

0   5m

Brown Residence

Lake | Flato Architects
Scottsdale, Arizona, USA

Despite being located in an expansive golf community, the Brown Residence revels in stunning desert views from almost every space. Its careful design makes this possible, as views to neighbouring houses are edited out, focused instead on distant mountains. While the residence presents an unassuming, modest scale to the street, it steps down with the slope of the site, allowing the spaces inside to become quite generous. Oversized pivot doors and large expanses of glass allow abundant light and air into these spaces, while broad overhangs and shading devices protect them from the harsh desert sun.

Simple stucco volumes play against the more voluminous steel and glass pavilion of the living and dining areas that anchors the site and creates a private courtyard. Concrete garden walls and concrete and stone hardscape define this courtyard and other exterior spaces. The concrete continues inside as the predominant floor material, while natural wood provides warmth on various wall, ceiling and floor surfaces throughout the house. A steel-clad swimming pool adjacent to the informal family room provides a pleasant escape from the desert heat.

Photography: Bill Timmerman

Floor plan

1 Entry
2 Living area
3 Dining area
4 Family area
5 Kitchen
6 Bedroom
7 Bathroom
8 Water closet
9 Walk-in wardrobe
10 Office
11 Guest bedroom
12 Guest ensuite
13 Firepit
14 Pool
15 Garage

0   4m

Bu Yeon Dang

IROJE KHM Architects
Sungmam, Gyeounggi-do, South Korea

This house is on an inclined and irregular plot in an urban environment, which the architect has tried to soften by creating a more rural setting. In order to maximise the efficiency of the plot, the irregular form of the site was adapted to fit the form of the architecture. As a result, the shape of site became the shape of architecture.

The house is a complex place, for both living and working. Because of this dual setting, the architect separated the building into an upper level and lower level, which separates the gate of the house and office along the level of an inclined access road. The open-plan structure eases vertical mobility and gives dramatic effect while producing visual and spatial continuity.

Floating wooden boxes are built into a small bamboo garden in the open space on each floor. The dynamic scenery of this inner space is the major impression of this complex house. By landscaping the entire rooftop of the house, the dramatic exterior space that is composed of various types – from underground level to the rooftop – is combined with dynamic indoor space and the surrounding scenery of nature, to produce a rich narrative.

The intention of harmonising the building within the surrounding context of nature, the flexible configuration of internal space, the curved line of the site and the vocabulary of architectural form combine to refine the non-architectural into something rather special.

Photography: Jong Oh Kim

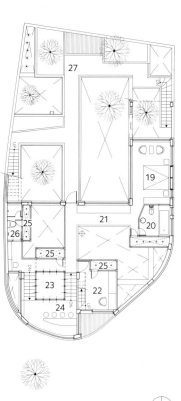

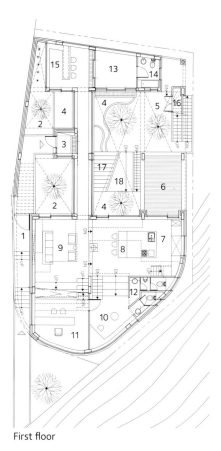

First floor

Second floor

0   3m

1 Gate
2 Entry courtyard
3 Entry
4 Pond
5 Inner courtyard
6 Deck
7 Kitchen
8 Dining area
9 Living area
10 Study
11 Office
12 Powder room
13 Guest bedroom
14 Guest ensuite
15 Bar
16 Boiler room
17 Waterfall
18 Inclined garden
19 Master bedroom
20 Master ensuite
21 Walk-through wardrobe
22 Children's study room
23 Family room
24 Bar
25 Bamboo garden
26 Water closet
27 Roof garden

Butternut Residence

House+House Architects
Hillsborough, California, USA

In a neighbourhood of traditional houses, this 750-square-metre (8,000 square feet) contemporary home is set deep into its lot with its garage, at 90 degrees to the street, to provide privacy and a choreographed arrival through a gracious front garden, enveloping this home in an aura of seclusion. Strong geometric forms interlocked with thick walls and broad bands of gridded windows are softened by gently vaulted roofs and an elegant palette of materials. Wide slate steps lead to a mahogany entry door set within a deep frame, bisecting the main gallery and continuing through to a swathe of luminous grass. Standing-seam roofing in a metallic champagne colour complements muted shades of taupe stucco.

A 7-metre-high (22 feet) sky-lit gallery floods this home with natural light, ending in framed views to flaming amber trees, allowing large windows to face neighbouring homes comfortably without window coverings. The living room and library are wrapped in thick, sculpted walls with a zigzag sweep of glass and mahogany pillars opening to distant views. The formal dining room is open yet set apart, with broad views toward front and rear gardens.

A secondary gallery links the garage and rear entry with the kitchen and family room. The sculpted stairway leads to the bedrooms, with a bridge flying through the double-height, sky-lit spaces to the master bedroom. High vaulted ceilings embrace each sleeping area, and clerestory windows allow sparkling sunlight to stream in throughout the day.

Photography: David Duncan Livingston

Ground floor

First floor

1 Entry
2 Living room
3 Library
4 Dining room
5 Kitchen
6 Family room
7 Bedroom
8 Utility room
9 Laundry
10 Work room
11 Recycling
12 Terrace
13 Garage
14 Master bedroom
15 Master bathroom
16 Dressing room
17 Study
18 Exercise room
19 Storage
20 Playroom

0   10m

Casa AA | Parque Humano
Mexico City, Mexico

This house was designed as a pavilion for observing and living in close proximity to nature. Organised around an open landscape, the result is an L-shaped plan one room wide – the intersection of the two axes radiates from the central living/dining area and all rooms flank the swimming pool and look out over surrounding parkland.

Pushing the limits of interior space through the use of floor-to-ceiling glass openings, the architect sought to bring house and landscape into a higher unity. More than just a composition of lines and planes, this residential design provides a framework for appreciating nature.

Through the use of a steel structure the architect created a greater feeling of lightness and openness. The use of overhangs provides shade and reduced glare. Brick is a fundamental material in the house and provides insulation during periods of extreme weather – primarily intense summer heat. The architect created a special composition where walls define space but do not bear weight.

The rectilinear composition is supported by a simple, geometric landscape design. The pool, while an obvious recreational asset, also serves to intensify the view from the interior by reflecting the changing colour of the sky and clouds.

Photography: Paul Rivera, ArchPhoto

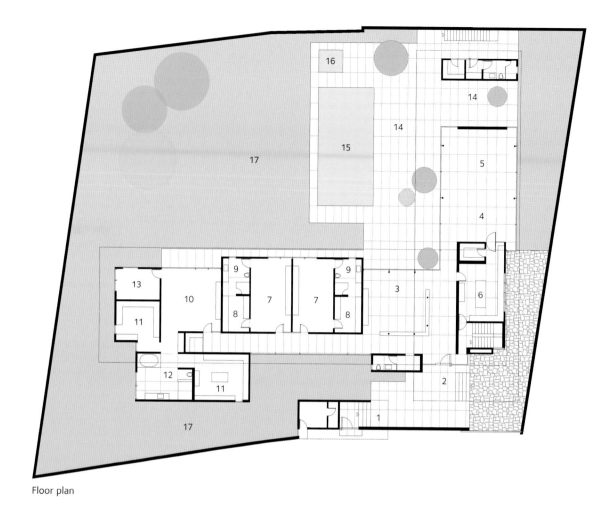

Floor plan

1 Courtyard
2 Entry
3 Family area
4 Dining area
5 Living area
6 Kitchen
7 Bedroom
8 Walk-in wardrobe
9 Ensuite
10 Master bedroom
11 Master walk-in wardrobe
12 Master ensuite
13 Study
14 Terrace
15 Pool
16 Jacuzzi
17 Garden

0   5m

Casa Diagonal

Safdie Rabines Architects
La Jolla, California, USA

This custom-built home is perched on a steep hillside site in La Jolla, southern California, overlooking the Pacific Ocean. The clients' only programmatic requirements were to consolidate all the main living spaces onto one level, and to create a simple, restrained design that ultimately 'paid homage' to the site. The width of the lot is perpendicular to the view, enabling the house to be completely oriented towards the ocean.

The residence takes advantage of its difficult site by carefully stepping down the hillside to create indoor–outdoor terraces on each level with panoramic views of the Pacific. The design uses a simple rectangular floor plate bisected by a diagonal wall running the length of the house. This wall pushes right up to the limits of the zoning envelope, allowing the main level to accommodate the owners' spatial requirements while maximising the views.

The exterior space created by the diagonal is 'captured' as a large outdoor terrace that effectively doubles the size of the interior living space. A steel staircase connecting the two levels is anchored by a two-storey stone wall and lit by a large skylight. A muted palette of concrete floor tiles, plaster, stone and walnut is used throughout the house, creating a serene space that defers to the surrounding context and provides a muted backdrop for the clients' collection of art.

Photography: Dennis Viera

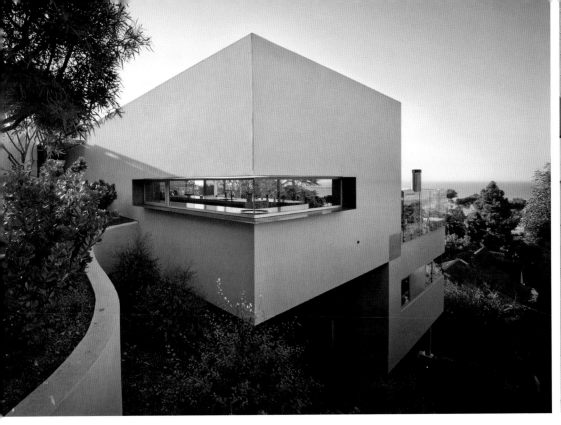

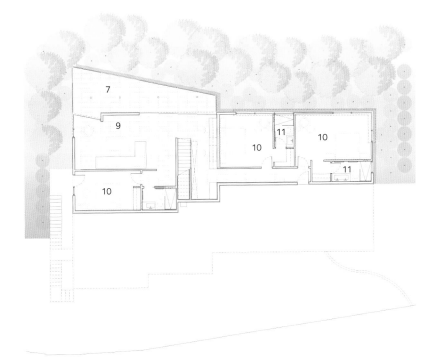

Ground floor

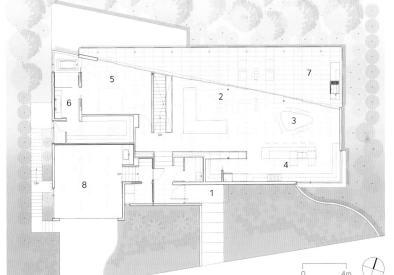

First floor

1 Entry
2 Living area
3 Dining area
4 Kitchen
5 Master bedroom
6 Master ensuite
7 Terrace
8 Garage
9 Study
10 Bedroom
11 Ensuite

0   4m

Casa Iseami

Robles Arquitectos
Principal: Juan Robles
Playa Carate, Puntarenas, Costa Rica

The house is the first physical manifestation of the ISEAMI Institute (Institute for Sustainability, Ecology, Art, Mind and Investigation). The house is the main area of the institute and it will serve as a multifunctional place hosting activities including research, meditation, training, yoga and relaxation, specifically on the first floor terrace.

The architect followed a design process that evaluates 10 important elements: site, climate, energy, water, materials, environment, atmosphere, cost, innovation with the use of passive strategies and implemented processes. These elements were analysed to develop a design and management plan during the building lifecycle in order to reduce the potentially negative effect the house could have on the natural environment; and conversely to minimise the negative effect nature could have on the building. In short, the architect's principal objective was to create an extremely low-maintenance house.

The secluded project site is located 30 kilometres from the nearest town, Puerto Jiménez, and the house does not have mains electricity or water. This required the Institute to invest in a house that is entirely self-sufficient for its energy and water needs.

The structural and electromechanic design was inspired by the exoskeleton of an insect. The creation of open spaces between walls and ceilings eliminates enclosed space, creating beneficial indoor air quality and avoiding the conditions for mould and infestation from insects – a common problem with projects in tropical climes. Passive design strategies have been successfully implemented to handle sun exposure, relative humidity, natural illumination and ventilation, according to bioclimatic circumstances.

Photography: Sergio Pucci

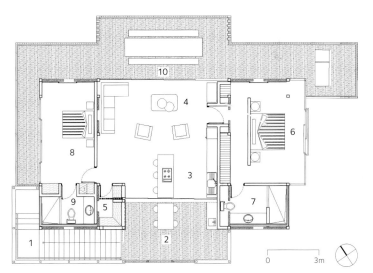

First floor

1 Staircase from ground floor
2 Dining area
3 Kitchen
4 Living area
5 Pantry
6 Master bedroom
7 Master ensuite
8 Bedroom
9 Ensuite
10 Deck

Casa La Roca

Parque Humano
Valle de Bravo, Mexico

For the concept of this project the architect took advantage of the triangular character of the plot, the slope of the land and the views towards Cerro Gordo nature reserve. The building has been conceived as a homogenous mass, hollowing out a huge opening with an inviting forced perspective effect caused by the asymmetric walls that frame the natural panorama. With the objective of building an interior–exterior relation, the volumetric setting of sloping walls and slabs allows the visual journey from the interior space, deeply linking the project to the landscape outside; it is the exterior landscape that organises interior spaces.

The house is developed in two volumes separated by a garden and connected by a bridge. Parking and service areas comprise the basement level. From here the stairs lead to the main entry. Within the first volume, the

architect placed the living and dining spaces and kitchen on the ground floor; bedrooms are located on the first floor. The subsequent volume hosts a working studio, facing the inner court. Each space has a proportion and a characteristic relationship with the adjacent space, as well as a relationship with the existing landscape.

The house overlooks the environment, incorporating the landscape, making an atmosphere of outdoor life and reconstructing the dynamic perception of space, with an emphasis on the emotional bonds between subject and nature. Working with nature is a way of working towards an understanding of the world.

Photography: Paul Rivera, ArchPhoto

48

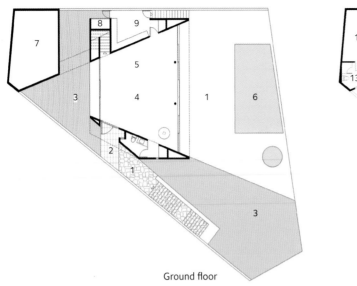

Ground floor

First floor

1 Terrace
2 Entry
3 Garden
4 Living area
5 Dining area
6 Pool
7 Studio
8 Cellar
9 Kitchen
10 Master bedroom
11 Master ensuite
12 Bedroom
13 Ensuite
14 Bridge

0   5m

Cedar Lake Home & Guesthouse

Charles R. Stinson Architects
Minneapolis, Minnesota, USA

For years this sloping site sat empty after a fire destroyed a 19th-century home, despite its striking views toward Cedar Lake and the downtown Minneapolis skyline. Originally the lot was subdivided and the architect envisaged three complementary compositions with a sense of loft living and a superb view, by lifting the main living quarters of each home to the second level. The first of the three designs was built and then purchased by a European couple who found the minimalist design synonymous with their modern lifestyle. Before finding this lot, the couple had searched for downtown lofts before realising they could get a similar urban feel from a home that also took advantage of the substantial lake and trail system that is unique to Minneapolis.

After settling into their new home, the couple purchased the property adjoining their lot. They revisited the architect with the aspiration of building a guesthouse to accommodate family members from overseas who visit for several months at a time. The couple also requested a swimming pool and large exterior entertainment space for gatherings. An additional kitchen and living room would serve both their long-stay guests, as well as allow seamless entertainment outside, around the new pool. Above the main living space, the loft bedroom would create stunning views through two storeys of glass facing the morning skyline and the verdant park beyond. The overall goal was to give a unique identity to the guesthouse, while maintaining a sense of cohesion with the original home.

Photography: Paul Crosby

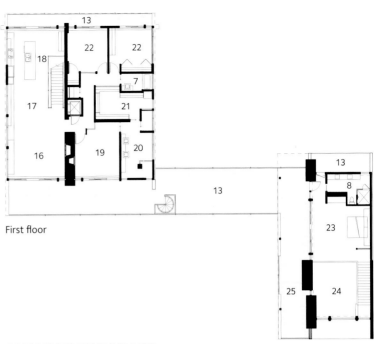

First floor

Ground floor

1 Main entry
2 Study
3 Media room
4 Laundry
5 Garage
6 Mudroom
7 Mechanical room
8 Bathroom
9 Recreation room
10 Glass link
11 Guest/pool kitchen
12 Guest living room
13 Deck

14 Fireplace and sitting area
15 Pool
16 Living area
17 Dining area
18 Kitchen
19 Master bedroom
20 Master ensuite
21 Master walk-in wardrobe
22 Bedroom
23 Guest loft
24 Void
25 Private sitting area

0   5m

55

Chenequa Residence

Robert Oshatz Architects
Chenequa, Wisconsin, USA

The architect was asked to design a home for a growing family on a heavily wooded site adjacent to a lake on Milwaukee's western fringe. A thin driveway meanders its way between cornfields and groves of elk trees before presenting itself on the house. From the approach, the house looks small. The radial floor plan wraps itself around the face of the sloping site and avoids all existing trees, reducing the house's scale and preventing it from ever being visible as a whole. The spiralling eco-roof that twists itself around the stone lift core also reduces the visual height of the building.

The main entry to the house is located under the lowest segment of the spiralling roof. Upon walking through the glass door, the compression of the low entry explodes into a celebration of light and form. A large circular opening in the floor exposes a new level below, while the low roof lifts and spins out of view and is followed by a cantilevered staircase. A solid stone core stands at the centre of it all, like a choreographer directing the dance around it.

The entry level accommodates the house's public spaces including the kitchen, lounge and dining room, while the lower floor is used for the family-oriented spaces. The level above the entry hosts the master bedroom, an ensuite and a nursery. A door opens out from the upper floor onto the roof, which is made up of a series of stepped roof terraces that overlook the lake and the surrounding landscape.

Oshatz believes providing connections between the internal spaces and the exterior environment is beneficial to the occupants' wellbeing. Frameless glazing provides unobstructed views throughout the house to the lake beyond. Natural materials are used to tie the house into its environment – quartz stone walls appear to grow out of the ground and hemlock ceilings blend with the exterior tree canopy. Materials are carried seamlessly through the glazing line to break down the definition between the interior and the exterior, ensuring an uninterrupted flow of space between inside and out. The result is a structure that is at peace with its environment and within which occupants are at peace with themselves.

Photography: Cameron Neilson

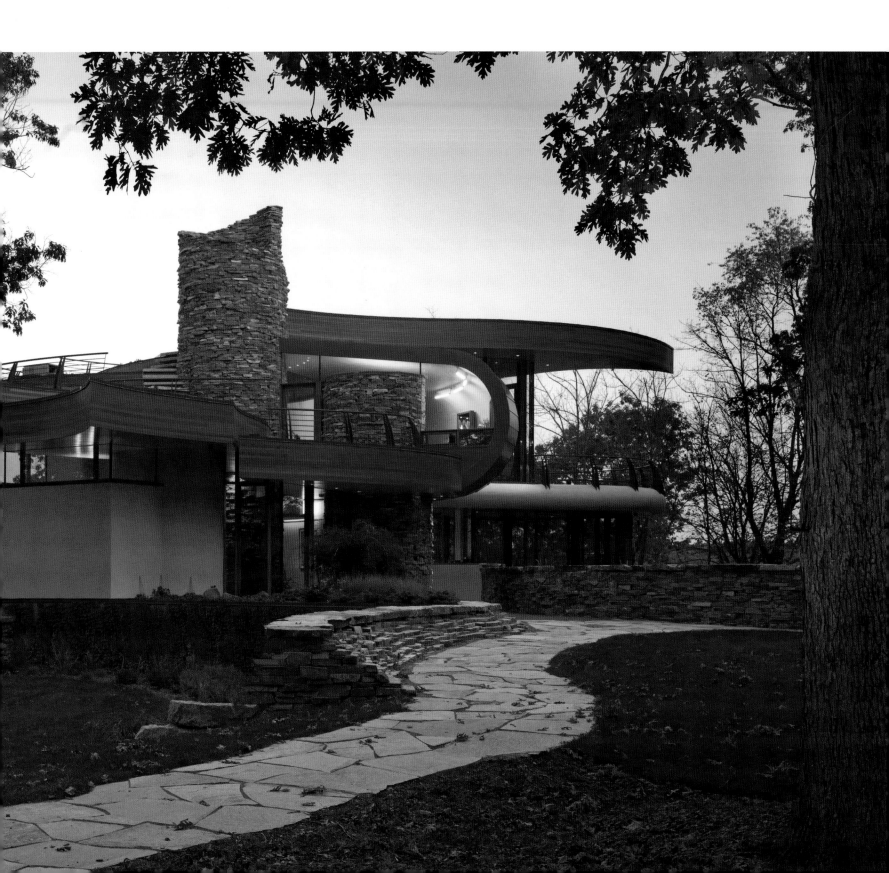

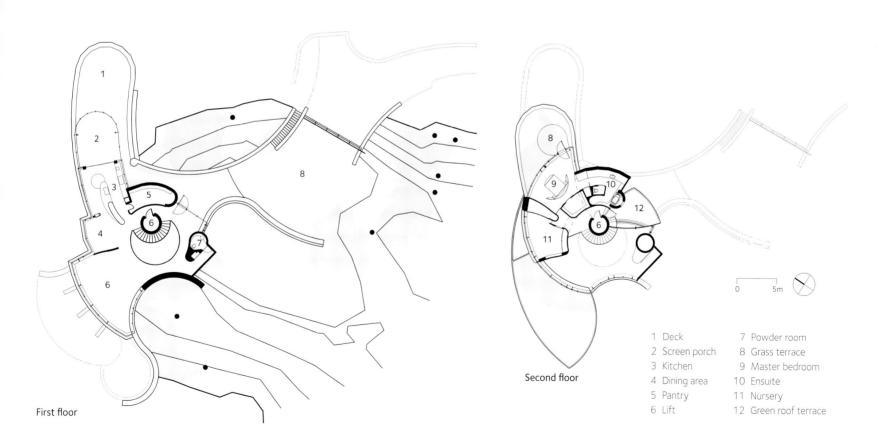

First floor

Second floor

1 Deck
2 Screen porch
3 Kitchen
4 Dining area
5 Pantry
6 Lift
7 Powder room
8 Grass terrace
9 Master bedroom
10 Ensuite
11 Nursery
12 Green roof terrace

Chesapeake Bay House

McInturff Architects
Neavitt, Maryland, USA

There is a pool on the roof of this house; and all the exterior elements are on high too – decks, porches and mechanical systems. The reason is simple: the site, a quiet cove in a waterman's village on Maryland's Eastern Shore, is subject to strict guidelines that protect Chesapeake Bay. The allowable footprint for everything on the site is restricted to the ruins of a long-gone house that has been excavated, surveyed and documented.

That earlier house was about the size of a double-width trailer, so the current home is all piled up, fitting on deck – like a modern-day Ark with 155 square metres (1650 square feet) of interior space. Given the height and weight to be supported, the structure is made of cross-braced steel moment frames that impose themselves and are on view throughout the plan.

The house, designed by the architect for himself, has an open-plan first floor with multiple sliding doors that turn the interior into a porch. A winding stair rises to two stacked bedrooms and continues to the roof-top pool. On the exterior, white cedar shingles and stainless steel will weather naturally, as there is no paint or stain on the outside. The interior is all white – simplicity itself.

Photography: Julia Heine

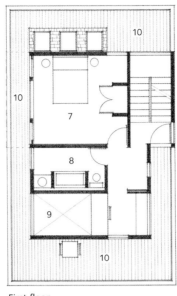

Ground floor

First floor

1 Entry
2 Sitting area
3 Dining area
4 Living area
5 Kitchen
6 Powder room
7 Bedroom
8 Bathroom
9 Double-height space
10 Deck

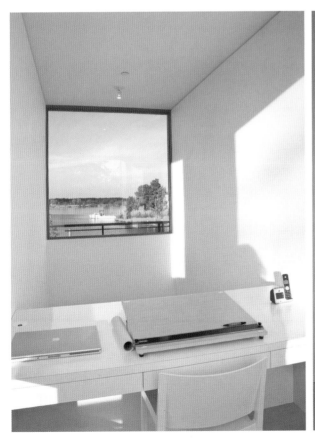

Cliff House

Architecture Saville Isaacs
Sydney, New South Wales, Australia

The architect's aim was to create a peaceful and healthy environment for the clients, to carefully construct a place to live in which everyday living is a joy and every simple function gives pause to reflect, by connecting each function to the surrounding nature; and to achieve this using ecologically sustainable development principles and sustainable, recycled, low or non-toxic and cost-effective materials. The overall layout and design of the house is practical and suitable for the needs of an older couple without children. Single car parking has been provided; the owners use the nearby railway to commute to the city.

Cost-effective, readily available and locally produced materials have been used in innovative ways with the raw beauty of the materials providing the sense of luxury, selected to ensure minimal impact on the greater environment, the local environment, as well as on the inhabitants' health. Materials used are standard components chosen to minimise embodied energy and cost. Compressed fibre cement is used for wall and floor finishes, while recycled timbers are used internally, with radially sawn plantation timbers used externally. Floors, walls, roof and ceilings are heavily insulated. Low-emission finishes were selected: laminates, rather than polyurethane, were employed for joinery; low-emission glues, paints and wax to seal timbers.

The design responds to the challenges of the south east-orientation, with windows strategically positioned to maximise winter sunlight penetration. Rainwater is captured for water closets, laundry and irrigation. Blackwater recycling was extensively investigated, but pump-out installed due to unstable geotechnical site conditions prevented water dispersal on site.

The house relies on sea breezes for cooling and a heat-pump hydronic system (there is no gas supply), augmented by wood fires, for space heating.

The built outcome was the result of an extensive process including the builder and structural, hydraulic and geotechnical engineers to resolve the significant challenges posed by the unstable cliff-edge site. The cantilevered architectural forms enable footings to be kept away from the eroding sides of the site.

The building is essentially galvanised steel, plasterboard, fibre cement sheeting, recycled timber and laminate joinery. How these materials are put together and expressed creates the quality of space and architecture.

Photography: Kata Bayer

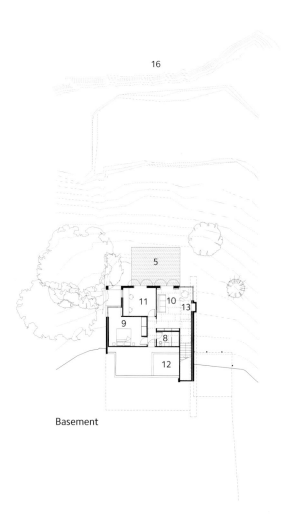

16

5

11 | 10 | 13

9

8

12

Basement

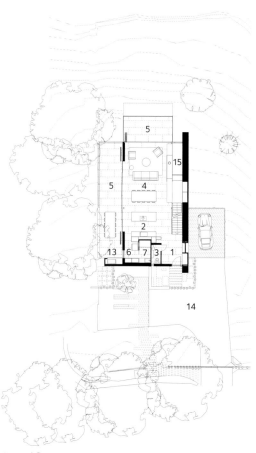

5

15

5

4

13 | 6 | 7 | 3 | 1

14

Ground floor

5

9

8

5

First floor

1 Entry	10 Library
2 Kitchen	11 Office
3 Powder room	12 Services
4 Living room/dining room	13 Fireplace
5 Deck/balcony	14 Driveway
6 Pantry	15 Void
7 Laundry	16 Cliff edge
8 Bathroom	
9 Bedroom	

0   5m

Clifton Hill House

Sharif Abraham Architects
Melbourne, Victoria, Australia

The site spans two streets and has two frontages. An original Art Deco house faced the main street. The client's brief was to refurbish this house, providing two new bathrooms and adding an open-plan living space to its rear. The architect sought to design an addition that was sympathetic to the original house, while advancing the stylistic and spatial qualities of its architectural style.

The addition is a collection of sculptural roof forms oriented to provide outlook and sunlight to the interior as well as responding to the setback regulations of the local building code. Made from concrete with fine stucco finish and aluminium edging, the walls are pierced by large sheets of glass and high windows, establishing transparency and lightness in the form and a sensitive relationship with the future garden. Between the addition and the original house, a new courtyard is located to provide light to the inner rooms and living spaces. A discreet staircase at one corner leads to an upper deck located between the roof forms to give panoramic views of treetops over the roof of the original house.

The interior spaces contrast curved black timber with white walls. Ceilings trace the inside of sculptural roof elements to create double-height spaces and then curve down to create intimate spaces. A linear element replicating the trunk of a tree extends the full width of a room, establishing visual continuity with the kitchen and the garden beyond. The timber (Ebony Macassar) is sourced from the trunk of a single tree. The outside of the trunk, where the grain is younger, is located high in the space and progressively descends to the joinery and intimate spaces where the core is dense and dark. The consistency of the application of the veneer to the upper portions of the walls is intended to make the living areas feel more intimate while maintaining the roof height needed to capture sunlight throughout the day.

A corridor with a continuous light beam emanating from its ceiling guides the inhabitants away from the addition and into the original house, leading to the two new bathrooms. The first bathroom is clad in black tiles and presents a dark cavernous experience by surfacing the floor, walls and ceiling with dark textured tiles. The darkness of the interior is intended to focus on the user's nude form. By contrast the other bathroom is open to the courtyard and is flooded with natural light. Continuous bronze tiles unify the space and accentuate natural light as it moves across their surfaces. The corridor and bathrooms are intended as counterpoints to the architecture of the original house, posing questions about the nature of old and new and suggesting possibilities for their reconciliation.

Photography: Matthew Stanton

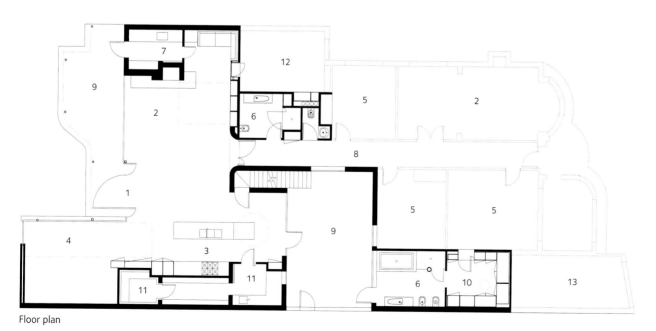

Floor plan

1 Entry
2 Living area
3 Kitchen
4 Dining room
5 Bedroom
6 Bathroom
7 Laundry
8 Corridor
9 Deck
10 Cupboards
11 Utility/store
12 Study
13 Garage

Coastal Residence

Boora Architects
The Oregon Coast, USA

This residence is an exploration in erasing boundaries between indoors and out. Located on the central Oregon coast, the 265-square-metre (2865 square feet) two-building home opens to the natural landscape, and offers 180-degree views. The design employs a duality of openness and expansive views with spaces that are both private and quiet.

The residence is organised into three parts, joined in U-shape formation around a central courtyard fronting the view. The upper floor in the largest of the two buildings is extensively glass-walled. Windows crescendo from 2.5 metres to 4.5 metres in height (8 feet to 15 feet) at the most outward-facing point.

A large covered deck extends the indoor footprint by an additional one-third, joining the massing of the residence, framing an outdoor invisible wall. The lower level is more private, with two bedrooms, two bathrooms and a flex room – a space that converts an open living area into a guest bedroom by pulling two 2.4-metre (8 feet) sliding hemlock accordion pocket panels to form walls.

Native dwarf shore pines shelter the lower level, affording necessary privacy. On the upper level, the experience is of suspension as one's feet are just slightly above the treeline.

The second building combines a 30-square-metre (295 square feet) office and bathroom with a garage below. A hybrid copper rooftop, formed by cross-pollinating the typology of a shed and dormer roof, forms an origami-joined ceiling in the office area. A 14-metre-long (45 feet) covered walkway sided in horizontal slats forms the base of the U-shape. The landscaped courtyard fuses building with walkway, creating focus on where interior and exterior spaces merge. At night, the residence appears as a lantern, and the central courtyard is its hearth.

Photography: Jon Jensen

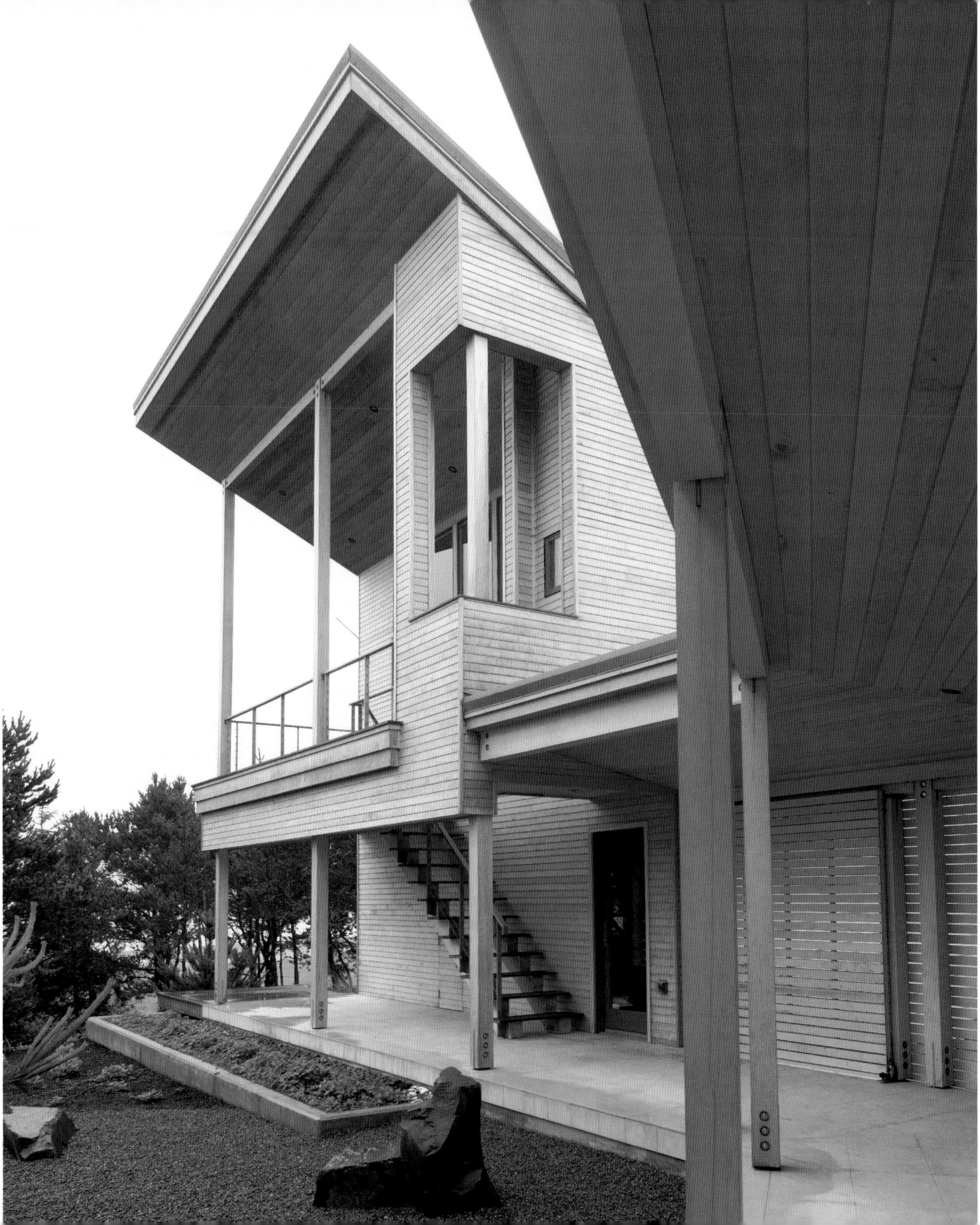

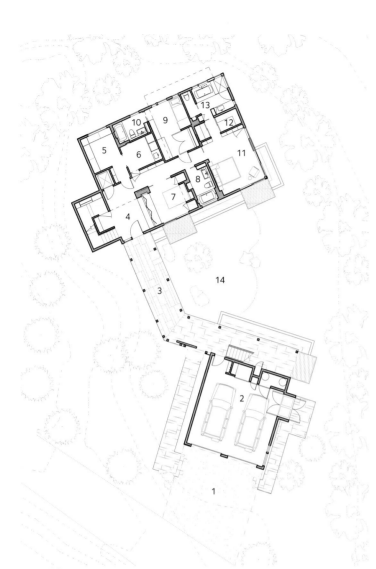

Ground floor

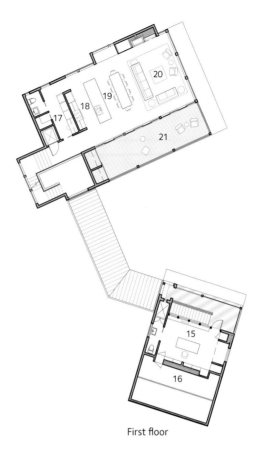

First floor

1 Driveway
2 Garage
3 Breezeway
4 Entry
5 Lounge
6 Laundry
7 Guest bedroom
8 Guest bathroom
9 Children's bedroom
10 Children's ensuite
11 Master bedroom
12 Walk-in wardrobe
13 Master ensuite
14 Courtyard
15 Office
16 Storage
17 Pantry
18 Kitchen
19 Dining room
20 Living room
21 Deck

0   4m

Coleman Residence

Iredale Pedersen Hook Architects
City Beach, Western Australia

The Coleman Residence explores the illusion of the home as a holiday retreat, exploiting the tapering boundaries with a vanishing point that meets in the neighbouring property. It engages with the possibility of spatial illusion resulting from the a-perspective approach to spatial construction and the relationship of the everyday experience of the family residence. The vanishing point is denied visibility by a wall at the end of the property that serves to exaggerate the illusion with an installation by artist Jurek Wybraniec.

Analogous to a wedge of Camembert cheese, the tactile and sensuous materials are reserved for the interior spaces and courtyards. The large, anonymous, external white walls resonate as powerful barriers, carefully concealing the internal richness of the private world.

All space is organised as a series of wedges that connect to the illusory vanishing point. These wedges collect interior and exterior space. Driving through the middle of the residence is a wedge of recycled Jarrah –

a large deck that starts at the street boundary and ends 1.5 metres (5 feet) back from the rear boundary. This wedge connects the interior and exterior, forming spaces of ambiguity and creating a resonating curved court that brings the exterior deep in to the interior.

Photography: Patrick Bingham-Hall and Peter Bennetts

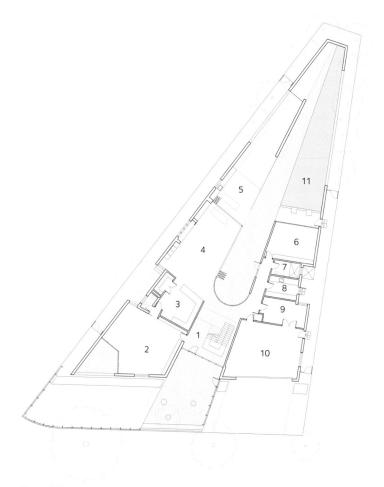

1 Entry
2 Study
3 Kitchen
4 Living room/dining area
5 Al fresco area
6 Rumpus room
7 Bathroom
8 Laundry
9 Store
10 Garage
11 Pool
12 Terrace
13 Bedroom
14 Water closet
15 Master bedroom
16 Walk-in wardrobe
17 Master ensuite
18 Gym

0   5m

Ground floor

First floor

Connecticut House

Austin Patterson Disston Architects
Long Island Sound, Connecticut, USA

Prominently poised on a hill with expansive views of Long Island Sound on a street aptly named Bluewater Lane, this new three-storey 950-square-metre (10,200 square feet) house has its design roots in Europe. The clients had lived in Europe with their young family and were drawn to gracious formality. The stucco, wrought-iron railings, steel windows and courtyard of their home present characteristics of a European country house. Yet the house and family who inhabit it are distinctly American.

With a site that embraces the water view, the design by partner McKee Patterson called for an informality that would mirror this young family's love for easy entertaining and connections to the outside terrace and pool. The house moves easily from the more formal

public spaces of the two living rooms with 3.7-metre (12 feet) ceilings and an extensive trim system, to the breakfast room and kitchen area with rusticated painted heavy timber beams and simple trim. All rooms facing the water feature French doors opening to the terrace, welcoming in gentle summer breezes.

The whole ground floor with both its formal and informal detailing is unified with its antiqued, hand-hewn, stained oak flooring that has been 'pillowed', giving it an Old World feel. The decor, by Heiberg Cummings Design of New York, mirrors its architecture with a combination of traditional and contemporary pieces. The design goal was to create rooms to be enjoyed and used everyday – not stuffy and off-putting.

Photography: Keith Scott Morton

First floor

28	29
	30 32
	31
	33
6 34	8 8
5	6 37 40
6	39 38 6
	33 41
	42
	6 10
	33
36	6 6 36
	35 35
	43

35 35 35
10 36 10 10 36

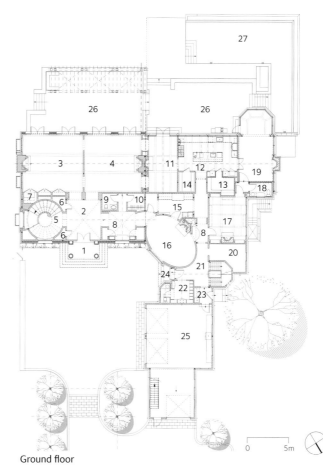

Ground floor

1 Front portico
2 Front hall
3 Living room
4 Family room
5 Main stair
6 Closet
7 Wet bar
8 Hall
9 Powder room
10 Water closet
11 Breakfast room
12 Kitchen
13 Pantry
14 Walk-in cooler
15 Butler's pantry
16 Dining room
17 Library
18 Changing room
19 Screen porch
20 Office
21 Back hall
22 Mud room
23 Potting room
24 Porch
25 Garage
26 Terrace
27 Pool
28 Master bedroom
29 Master bathroom
30 Shower
31 His walk-in wardrobe
32 Her walk-in wardrobe
33 Vestibule
34 Gallery
35 Bedroom
36 Ensuite
37 Guest bedroom
38 Dressing room
39 Guest bathroom
40 Family room
41 Laundry
42 Linen closet
43 Playroom

0   5m

Conservatory House

Ignatov Architects
Varna, Bulgaria

Conservatory House is a place for relaxation through enjoyment of natural serenity and the arts. The brief called for a customised, green, disabled-accessible residence with a large flower conservatory also suitable for hosting musical performances. Inspired by local trees, the new structure fills a void from an old sand quarry, reinforcing the terrain around it and branching out to accommodate the programme.

The conservatory music room is placed on top of the residence in order to catch maximum sunlight and offer the best views – views which comprise a prominent feature of the room. It welcomes family and guests and provides disabled guests with access to all levels. The carbon footprint is minimised by utilising an advanced geothermal system that covers all heating and cooling needs of the house and benefits from the insulating effect of the conservatory. The system cleanly and quietly exchanges thermal energy with earth via six 100-metre-deep (330 feet) closed-loop probes paired with a heat pump that requires minimal power to run. Hot water is supplied by a 500-litre (130 gallons) boiler coupled with the heating system and an array of solar vacuum tubes integrated into the glazed roof. Rainwater is collected for irrigation and waste water is treated on-site by a bioactive purification unit.

The reinforced concrete structure is chosen because of its thermal mass and sculptural presence. Façade diagonals follow the shortest stress-lines and reveal the structural tectonics. Set in this way, the house works like a tree with a green crown (the conservatory), a trunk (the elevator core), branches (the underlying structure) and roots (geothermal probes), with the residential pockets nested in symbiosis with it. Recent performance results show that Conservatory House consumes very little external power. Its design actively promotes environmental awareness in a new architectural language, combined with advanced engineering solutions.

Photography: Boris Ignatov, Rossen Donev

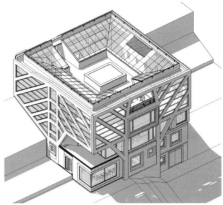

Solar roof

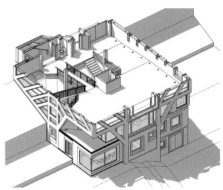

Conservatory

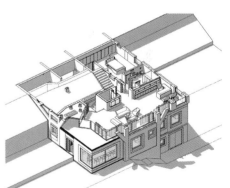

First floor

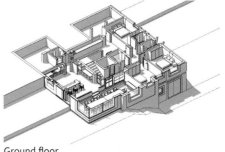

Ground floor

Crowsnest House

Phorm Architecture + Design
Agnes Waters, Queensland, Australia

Crownest House is perched above the township of Agnes Waters and 1770 on Queensland's Discovery Coast. It commands a view to Rocky Point and the last surf beach on the eastern coastline of Australia before the surf surrenders to the Great Barrier Reef. It was designed as a retreat for a young couple and as a place to host friends and family.

The house coils around itself on the top of the hill, with the bedroom tower anchoring onto a rocky outcrop and living quarters cantilevered off the hillside. The plan responds to intense mapping and interlocution with the broader site. The form creates a central private deck that addresses the principal view and panoramic sweep. Open to the night sky, the deck relies on 'shadow-casting' from the deck awning and the massing of the house to shade and protect. The east-facing timber-screened wall modulates the morning light and becomes a lit canvas at day's end. The timbers will be allowed to age to a silver grey with the passing of time.

The interiors form a chain of relaxed coastal volumes, tempered from the intense tropical light. Expressed detailing in local hardwoods and timber veneers contrast with articulated white plaster and polished concrete. Movement through the interior of the house is choreographed to reveal selected views of landscape. The clients have noted that the interiors are akin to 'living inside a musical instrument', inspiring raised voice and song.

Journeying through the house one finally arrives at the 'crow's nest'. Like a pulpit addressing the sea, the cantilevered white cube projects beyond the edge of the house, leaving one to hover in the breeze, looking out to the blue horizon.

Photography: Keith Burt

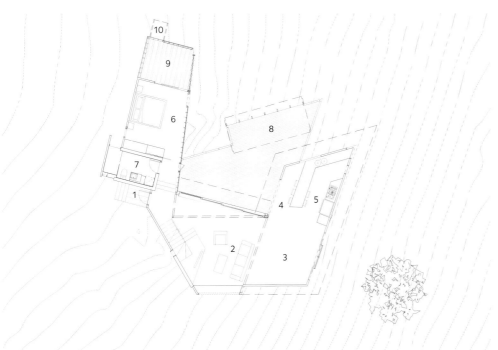

Ground floor

1 Entry	6 Bedroom
2 Living area	7 Ensuite
3 Dining area	8 Balcony
4 Breakfast bar	9 Deck
5 Kitchen	10 Crow's nest

0   3m

The Cruciform

studio 101 architects
Mount Macedon, Victoria, Australia

This substantial home designed for a large family is located in the expansive rural landscape of Mount Macedon. With magnificent views of the surrounding mountain ranges and the monumental war memorial, the sizeable programmatic requirements were crafted into a linear 'cruciform' plan maximising the outlook and northern orientation.

Glimpsed from a meandering driveway, the residence appears through the dappled light of the dense bushland. One is led to the entry along a spine wall of local sandstone that continues through the house, acting as a thermal mass wall and spatially as a central organising element. The lower level contains the ancillary spaces of garage, storage, home office and a cabana room. On the upper level, the central zone handles the family and entertaining spaces. The eastern wing contains five bedrooms, all with framed views to the north; the primary living zone is housed in the western wing, containing an open-plan kitchen, dining area and lounge.

The building form hovers above the landscape on a recessive masonry podium. The upper level runs perpendicular to the natural topography, culminating in a dramatic cantilever to the west. The solidity of the ground-level masonry and stone acts as a counterbalance to the upper-level lightweight-clad forms, maximising the view, ventilation and exposure to the northern orientation. The crisp skillion roofline above the primary living zone floats above a ring of high-level glazing and is pitched to frame and reflect the mountain ranges; it folds down to the west, acting as a shield from the afternoon sun like the brim of a well-worn Akubra, or Australian bush hat.

A pre-fabricated skeletal steel frame is expressed both internally and externally, and provides the structure for each of the forms to be wrapped in an honest palette of natural materials. These include ironbark timber, copper cladding, glass and local sandstone. Each material has been carefully selected to evolve with time and work up a graceful patina of age. A sustainable design solution, sensitive to the site, has allowed peaceful integration of the home with the surrounding landscape and serenity of the Macedon mountain range.

Photography: Trevor Mein

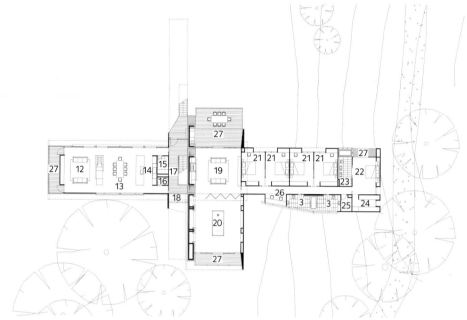

First floor

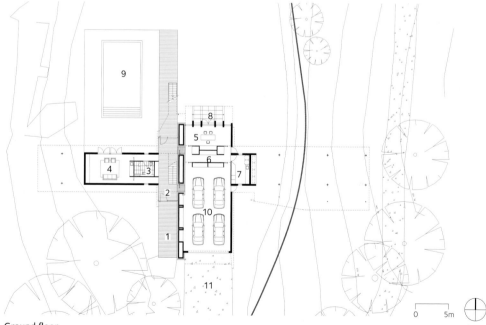

Ground floor

1 Entry deck	8 Terrace	15 Pantry	22 Master bedroom
2 Entry foyer	9 Pool	16 Powder room	23 Ensuite
3 Bathroom	10 Garage	17 Gallery space	24 Walk-in wardrobe
4 Pool cabana	11 Driveway	18 Void	25 Linen store
5 Office	12 Lounge	19 Living area	26 Study
6 Store	13 Dining area	20 Games room	27 Deck
7 Laundry	14 Kitchen	21 Bedroom	

Desert House

Lake | Flato Architects
Santa Fe, New Mexico, USA

Located north of Santa Fe in desert terrain, this house is a modern interpretation of a hacienda. It forms courtyards with low east–west-lying buildings linked by outdoor-oriented loggias and porches. The house is sheltered by being built into the hillside, leaving exposed concrete retaining walls, as well as insulating block solar mass walls that reach out to define space. The house has south-facing clerestories for passive solar gain and glazing on the north, east and west faces is minimised: the proportion of glass to wall is about one-third on the main house and the guesthouse and around one-quarter on the caretaker's house.

Housing the owner's art collection are a series of galleries of varying scales, lit by natural light, that address the variety of art and provide video-installation niches and walls that conceal technical equipment. The house has exposed-concrete radiant heated floors and the porches and overhangs are designed to provide shade from the southern sun, with east–west glass maximising winter heat gain. The house is designed for passive cooling to capture desert breezes at night, while forming a barrier to desert heat by day. An exterior-mounted west louvre in the living room controls glare and heat gain from the west, while preserving the panoramic view to the Sangre de Cristo mountains.

Photography: Frank Ooms

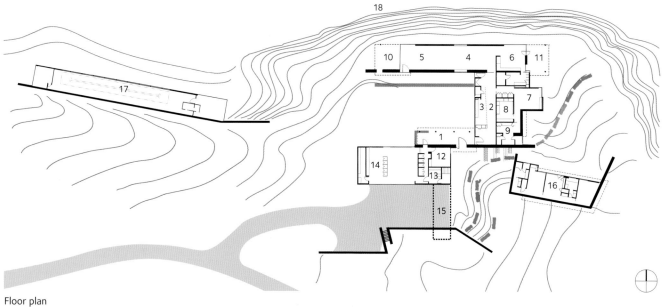

Floor plan

1 Entry loggia
2 Gallery
3 Office
4 Dining area
5 Living area
6 Kitchen
7 Master bedroom
8 Master walk-in wardrobe
9 Master ensuite
10 Sunset porch
11 Sunrise porch
12 Exercise room
13 Utility room
14 Garage
15 Caretaker quarters above
16 Guest quarters
17 Poolhouse
18 Cliff edge

Dillon Road

Base Architecture
The Gap, Queensland, Australia

Conceived from the bones of a brilliant, simple yet functional house belonging to renowned architect Geoffrey Pie, Dillon Road has grown into a contemporary piece of architecture that sits well within its place and serves the new owners, a family with four children.

A strict structural grid formed the basis for the expansion and an easy tectonic approach to the additional spaces. The orientation of the main and existing living wing was appropriate in the setting, with vast views perched on the top of the hill. A new wing comprising the children's sleeping quarters 'juts' out over an edge in the form of a glass box that captures its own secluded and isolated views.

As the general way we live has evolved and spread to the exteriors in this climate, new spaces that are both visual and extensions of the house's interiors are realised. A former corner kitchen has transformed into the heart of the house that spills to all sides and facilitates the outdoor living experience around the pool and surrounds, the pool being not only a focal point but also the linking element to what has become a very long house.

A mixture of good structure, sensible planning and a contemporary twist has revived this house into its second stage of life. The original materials of timber weatherboard and concrete blockwork have been retained externally. Polished concrete is carried through the house internally and externally, with a simple neutral colour scheme complemented by solid timber features, both inside and out.

Photography: Christopher Frederick Jones

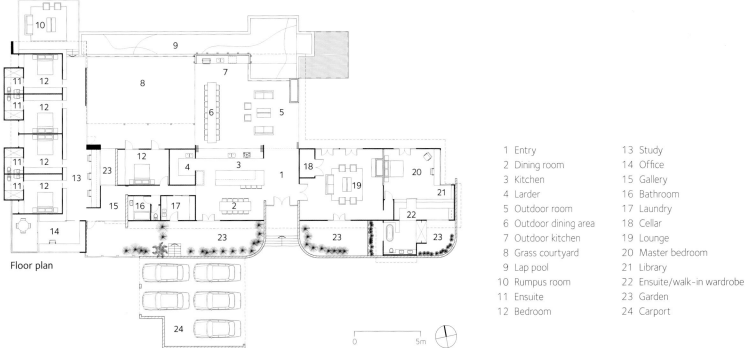

Floor plan

1 Entry	13 Study
2 Dining room	14 Office
3 Kitchen	15 Gallery
4 Larder	16 Bathroom
5 Outdoor room	17 Laundry
6 Outdoor dining area	18 Cellar
7 Outdoor kitchen	19 Lounge
8 Grass courtyard	20 Master bedroom
9 Lap pool	21 Library
10 Rumpus room	22 Ensuite/walk-in wardrobe
11 Ensuite	23 Garden
12 Bedroom	24 Carport

0   5m

Domeikava House

Vilius ir partneriai
Domeikava, Kaunas, Lithuania

The plastic shapes of curved lines always fit harmoniously into their environment. This recently realised project by Vilius ir partneriai confirms the truth of that statement. When looking from the slope, the laconic shape of the building seems to float in the air, hardly touching the ground with its glass surfaces. The building appears closed from the driveway, but on approach it reveals its integrated glass surfaces. For the curved shapes, the architects have used Twinson Face, a mixture of Deceunink NV timber and PVC, which creates exceptional aesthetics and is easy to maintain.

Inside, curved lines dominate not only the structure of the building, but also interior elements, including lights, shelves and integrated antechamber furniture. From the corridor one accesses the children's room, the master bedroom, the study and the bathroom and sauna. From here one enters the terrace, containing a small round plunge pool. A spacious cloakroom is situated next to the master bedroom.

The main area of the house consists of the sitting room, the dining room and the kitchen zone, framed by large windows lightly covered with black day curtains.

The curved glass surfaces expand the space and draw the line between the interior and natural surroundings. To create intimacy in the evening, the windows are covered with silk curtains. The sitting room is separated from other areas by an openwork set of shelves. In the fireplace area the architects have introduced a decorative wall made from ceramic Viva tiles. The laconic architecture throughout is filled with refined elegance and contemporary stylish luxury.

Photography: Raimondas Urbakavičius

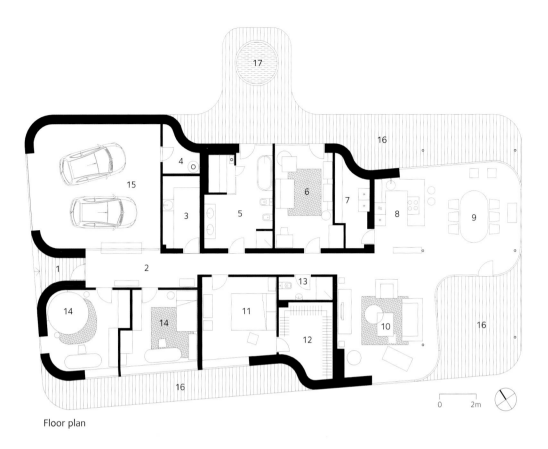

Floor plan

1 Entry
2 Hall
3 Laundry
4 Utility room
5 Bathroom/sauna
6 Guest bedroom
7 Store
8 Kitchen
9 Dining area
10 Living area
11 Master bedroom
12 Walk-in wardrobe
13 Water closet
14 Bedroom
15 Garage
16 Terrace
17 Plunge pool

0   2m

Dune House

Jarmund/Vigsnæs AS Architects
Thorpeness, Suffolk, UK

Dune House is situated in Thorpeness on the Suffolk coast, in the east of England, and replaced an existing building on the site. The house is a holiday home for rental and was commissioned by Living Architecture, a social enterprise founded to revolutionise architecture in the British holiday rental sector.

In order to receive planning permission it was important to relate to the existing, typical British seaside strip of houses. The roofscape – the bedroom floor – somehow plays with the formal presence of these buildings, and

also brings to mind a romantic remembrance of holidays at bed-and-breakfasts while travelling through Britain.

The ground floor contrasts this by its lack of relationship to the architecture of the top floor. The architectural ambiguity of the house also addresses the programmatic difference between the private upper floor and the social ground floor. The living area and the terraces are set into the dunes in order to protect them from the strong winds, and open equally in all directions to allow for wide, sweeping views of the coastal area and sea.

The corners can be opened by sliding doors, which emphasises the floating appearance of the top floor. While the materiality of the ground floor – concrete, glass and aluminium – relates to the masses of the ground, the upper floor is a construction made from solid wood, and the cladding is stained dark to match the existing gables and sheds found in the local area.

Photography: Nils Petter Dale

Ground floor

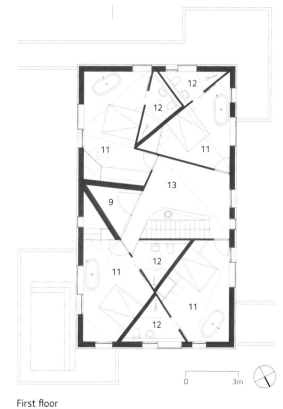

First floor

1 Entry
2 Day bed
3 Technology room
4 Living area
5 Dining area
6 Kitchen
7 Water closet
8 Bathroom
9 Terrace
10 Barbecue
11 Bedroom
12 Ensuite
13 Library

0   3m

Enclave House

BKK Architects
Melbourne, Victoria, Australia

This project was undertaken for a couple and their children of varying ages. It includes alterations to an existing Edwardian House and a new separate studio at the rear of the site. A central courtyard contains a pool and landscaped areas. The house is designed so that the spaces within and around the house will be adaptable over time to suit the changing needs of the family. The possibility for the studio space to be converted into an office has been considered, as has the basement entertainment area conversion into a gym or multi-purpose playroom.

The environmental initiatives for the project can be summarised as follows: there is a 25,000-litre (6600 gallons) underground tank for harvesting rainwater; double-glazed windows throughout; highly insulated walls, floors and roof; locally resourced, sustainable plantation timber-cladding; low-maintenance and low-VOC materials with inherent finishes; and highly water-efficient fixtures and fittings.

Formally, the extension at the rear of the existing residence is conceived through a subtractive approach that appears to have been carved from a solid block, chiseled away to comply with planning and heritage overlays, while also drawing light back into the residence. Deep reveals form the windows to the upper floor to protect the gaze from the surrounding residences. An interior lightwell and water feature extend the garden space to the centre of the living spaces. The existing garden has been carefully crafted to create its own secret garden, complete with designer cubby house.

There is an overwhelming sense of seclusion in both the house and garden that creates a type of space that is the family's own – a retreat from busy lives and the surrounding chaos of urban life. The fabric of the buildings operates like a protective cocoon, and the differing materiality of the two levels of the extensions creates the impression that the house has been capped or that a 'helmet' is placed upon the exterior walls.

Photography: John Wheatley, UA Creative

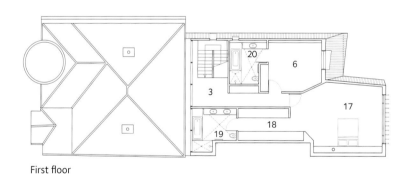

First floor

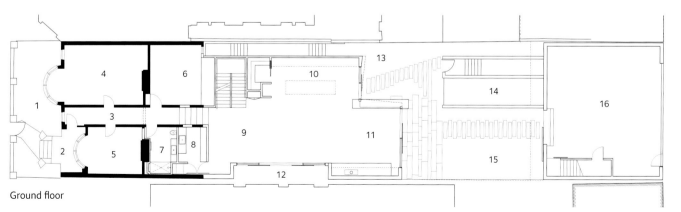

Ground floor

1 Garden
2 Entry
3 Hall
4 Studio
5 Study
6 Bedroom
7 Bathroom
8 Laundry
9 Dining area
10 Kitchen
11 Living area
12 Courtyard garden
13 Courtyard
14 Pool
15 Garden
16 Garage
17 Master bedroom
18 Walk-in wardrobe
19 Master ensuite
20 Ensuite
21 Studio
22 Studio bedroom
23 Kitchenette

0   3m

Fairfield Manor

Harrison Design Associates
Atlanta, Georgia, USA

True to the Regency style of early 19th-century Britain, this 1000-square-metre (11,000 square feet) private residence pays homage to the classical ideals of Ancient Greece and Rome. An intentional lack of exterior ornamentation emphasises the thoughtful scale, balance and proportion of the classical five-part structure. A palette of mahogany, cut limestone and thickly coated brick reflects solidity and refinement. Subtle details such as the decorative design found on the home's circular windows and iron railings reinforce the orderly aesthetics of the Regency period. The clean lines and simple forms of the interior architecture and furnishings serve to create a cohesive whole.

The entrance portico's four classical columns bring a lightness to the home's formal mass. The entry foyer's Regency style is evident in the Grecian medallion inset into the grey and buff limestone floor, the Greek key pattern and the delicate ironwork on the stair banister. The formal salon is accented with an elegant Greek frieze, replicated from a design by Sir John Soane (1753–1837). The dining room is anchored on one wall by a classically proportioned marble fireplace mantle. A floating staircase connects all three levels of the home. The space is filled with light from multiple windows; scored plaster walls create additional visual interest.

The gallery features a Doric colonnade marking the entrance to the salon. A forced perspective created by the thickened chevron pattern in the limestone flooring and fanlight transoms above doorways delineate the main block of the home. Custom mahogany French doors lead from the study out to the front terrace. Two loggias tucked into the wings of the house act as outdoor rooms overlooking the pool. The corners of the loggias are finished with masonry pilasters, giving them presence and underscoring the importance of balance as a key factor in the overall design.

A private courtyard off the master bedroom incorporates the circle-and-cross ironwork detail as a decorative element in this exterior space. Circular stone patterns underfoot further emphasise this unifying design feature. Small round windows – typical Regency style – are repeated on the front and rear of the home. The circle-and-cross details within the windows are replicated on the iron balustrading of the upper-level terrace. Balance, scale and proportion are reflected in the home's natural and built environment.

Photography: John Umberger

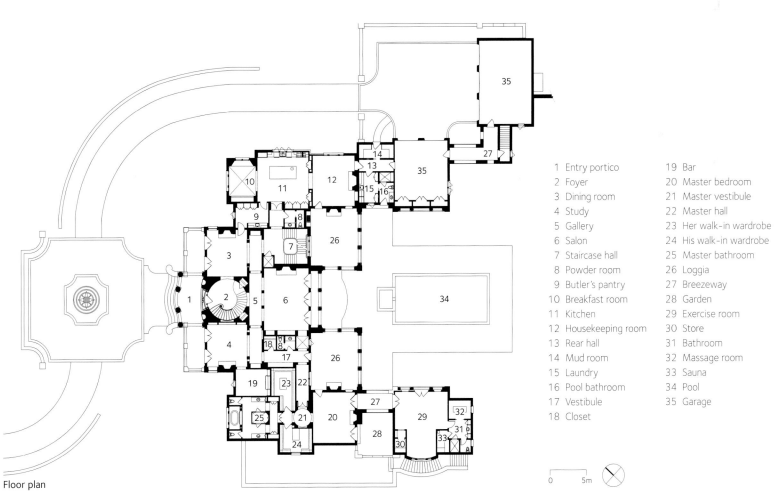

Floor plan

1	Entry portico	19	Bar
2	Foyer	20	Master bedroom
3	Dining room	21	Master vestibule
4	Study	22	Master hall
5	Gallery	23	Her walk-in wardrobe
6	Salon	24	His walk-in wardrobe
7	Staircase hall	25	Master bathroom
8	Powder room	26	Loggia
9	Butler's pantry	27	Breezeway
10	Breakfast room	28	Garden
11	Kitchen	29	Exercise room
12	Housekeeping room	30	Store
13	Rear hall	31	Bathroom
14	Mud room	32	Massage room
15	Laundry	33	Sauna
16	Pool bathroom	34	Pool
17	Vestibule	35	Garage
18	Closet		

0   5m

Fairway House

Max Pritchard Architect
Goolwa, South Australia

Located in a quiet seaside town in South Australia, this relaxed yet sculpture-like holiday house opens out to expansive views of a local golf course. The house presents a distinctive wave of timber battens to the street; this screen encloses the garage and forms an elevated entrance forecourt. The bright green garage door and entrance gate are vibrant insertions within this screen.

From this intermediate level a glass link connects the garage to the house, with a half-flight of stairs leading up to the main living area and bedroom, and down to another living area and two further bedrooms. A balcony and deck on each level maximise the indoor–outdoor feeling.

The two-storey design responds well to the site, utilising the slope of the land and maximising views and northern winter sun to living areas and bedrooms. The timber windows and doors are double-glazed, further improving thermal performance. In summer, sliding doors, banks of louvres and ceiling fans allow cross-ventilation to aid cooling. The north-sloping roof is well suited for the solar hot water system.

A limited palette of materials and clean detailing reinforce the relaxed atmosphere. Timber windows, floors, decking and bench-tops contrast with white walls and cabinetwork. Black strips in the laminated timber bench-tops recall boat decking and match the pattern of the external timber battens and decking elements. All roof water is collected for reuse and efficient waste-water treatment irrigates the garden, which is thickly planted with indigenous species.

Photography: Sam Noonan

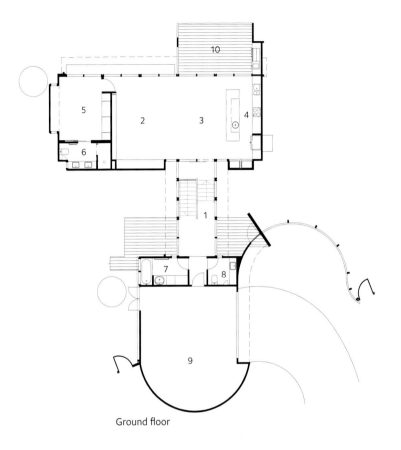

Ground floor

Lower ground floor

1 Entry
2 Lounge
3 Dining area
4 Kitchen
5 Bedroom
6 Ensuite
7 Bathroom/laundry
8 Water closet
9 Garage/store
10 Deck
11 Rumpus room
12 Bathroom
13 Balcony

0   3m

115

Florida Beach House

Iredale Pedersen Hook Architects
Florida Beach, Western Australia

The design of this holiday house one hour's drive from Perth emphasises the immensity of the Indian Ocean. All space is aligned and extruded through a strict dialogue of plan and section revealing the intensity and variety of this great ocean. The architect was interested in the rapidly disappearing holiday homes that once dominated the nearby landscape, houses that embodied the weekender experience designed with restraint, economy and robustness. This house captures these dying qualities, while screening the occupants from the emerging suburban houses and protecting them from strong winds and storms. A deck is created on each of the cardinal points, allowing the occupants to live externally any time of the year.

The reference point for the design was found in a sketch by the great Danish architect Jørn Utzon (best known for designing the Sydney Opera House), an image of people congregating on the beach under the dense, stormy Copenhagen sky. Uzton translated this into the section of a church, creating a mystical interior; the architect translated this into the section of a holiday house that intensifies the experience of the ocean.

The section undulates in relationship to the plan form; each space includes an undulation that is eventually revealed on the beach side as a series of undulations connecting the living, dining and kitchen spaces to the dynamic ocean environment. The section extrudes from the beach end to the street side; those spaces that do not contain a direct view to the ocean maintain the memory of the ocean view through the continuing section.

External cladding consists of a strictly controlled ribbon of uncut compressed fibre-cement sheeting and rough-sawn plywood panels. While the exterior is tactile and articulated, the interior is smooth and sculptured, with subtle variations of white paint colour and gloss levels differentiating interior elements and reflecting the exterior. A continuous band of high-performance glass articulates the wall-cladding from the roof, which is carefully sized to exclude summer sun yet admit low-level winter sun. The stretched western overhang excludes the low-level sun, allowing the occupants to engage in comfort with the setting sun.

The house appears to hover gently above the ground; a recessed concrete platform creates this illusion, connecting the house to the remaining holiday houses and the Dawesville Cut bridge. Constructed almost entirely from plantation pine timber, prefabricated and transported to Florida, the raw structure appears like the carcass of a great whale. The use of steel is minimised to a few select areas where thin columns support the dense undulating roof, creating tension in the context of the ocean view. The hovering platform is finished with recycled Jarrah and continues between the interiors and exterior as one large plane.

Photography: Peter Bennetts

Floor plan

1 Entry patio
2 Entry
3 Hall/gallery
4 Kitchen
5 Dining area
6 Living area
7 Study
8 Bedroom
9 Ensuite

10 Walk-in wardrobe
11 Study
12 Laundry
13 Water closet
14 Store
15 Shower room
16 Guest bedroom
17 Patio
18 Garage

0   4m

G+S+R House

Filippo Caprioglio
Caprioglio Associati Studio di Architettura
Monfumo, Treviso, Italy

The complex comprises two buildings that constitute a well-preserved historical farmhouse in the countryside of north-east Italy. The buildings lie adjacent to each other and are linked by an underground area housing the cellar and giving direct access from the house to the garage. The domestic building extends in linear fashion towards the old granary on the ground floor through a system of stairs and a catwalk on the first floor, from which there is access to the attic. The internal partition was conceived and realised to reference the original role of the building as a farmhouse, with particular attention to the relationship between interior and exterior.

Through the basement, where the cellar is located, is access to the garage excavated under the hill. The restoration of the domestic portion of the house was done in conservative fashion, respecting the original position of the doors and windows and preserving existing materials such as the original local yellow stone. The rural annex has been preserved for its structure but panelled in contemporary style, with teak wood employed for the exterior. The cube that hosts part of the kitchen is also panelled in teak.

The ground floor of the house is connected to the upper storey by a free-standing glass and steel staircase. A thin metal stairway then leads up to the loft, which is

designed as a wellness centre, bathroom and extensive wardrobe space. Operating in such a morphologically defined environment, all the work relative to the external conditions was made with great respect for the surrounding landscape without altering the underlying structure of the buildings.

Photography: Paolo Belvedere

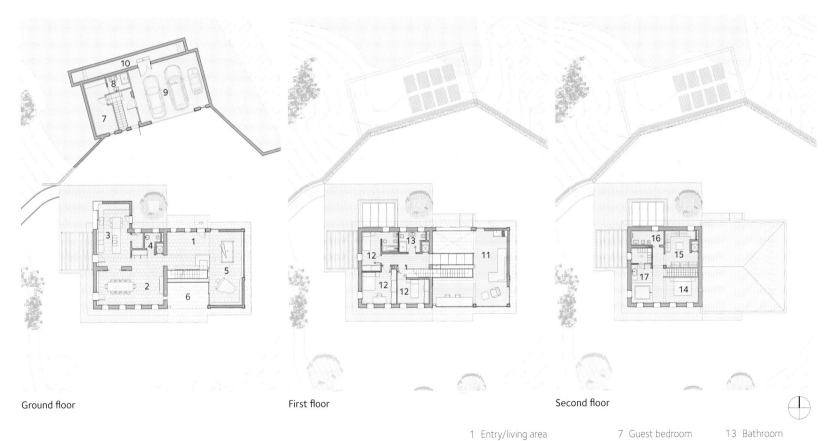

Ground floor

First floor

Second floor

1 Entry/living area	7 Guest bedroom	13 Bathroom
2 Dining area	8 Ensuite	14 Master bedroom
3 Kitchen	9 Garage	15 Walk-in wardrobe
4 Powder room	10 Mechanical room	16 Master ensuite
5 Games room/music room	11 Living area/studio	17 Steamroom
6 Lodge	12 Bedroom	

Glass House Mountains Residence

Bark Design Architects
Maleny, Queensland, Australia

The Glass House Mountains Residence celebrates its site, perched on the edge of the remnant rim of the Glass House range, as well as the essence of its place – sky and mountains. Translated into a place of 'glass and stone' inextricably connected to its landscape, it has qualities of being anchored, robust and earthbound as well as being transparent, light and floating.

Memorable to the experience is the 'sanctuary' of the courtyard space, whose edges are defined by ambiguous indoor–outdoor thresholds of the transparent internal spaces, sitting between the refuge of a monumental basalt 'garden wall' and the broader natural volcanic landscape. Engaging with existing topography, orientation, views and vegetation, the house balances economy and fine craft. Surfaces, finishes and details exhibit the Japanese concept of *wabi sabi* – the beauty of things imperfect, impermanent and incomplete, allowed to weather and evolve with time.

Sustainability starts with natural cooling and lighting, harnessing available breezes and winter sun, using locally sourced hardwood, plantation-grown plywood cladding and lining, recycled Blackbutt timber floors, local quarry rock and endemic garden species.

The house is separated into distinct spatial zones; and the feeling of pavilions connected around the edges of the courtyard creates the loosely connected village feel of a mountain lodge. Essential to the character of site is the landscape architecture, particularly the embued Gabion stone wall, which evolved into a personally placed element by the stonemason, and the crafted timber joinery.

Photography: Christopher Frederick Jones

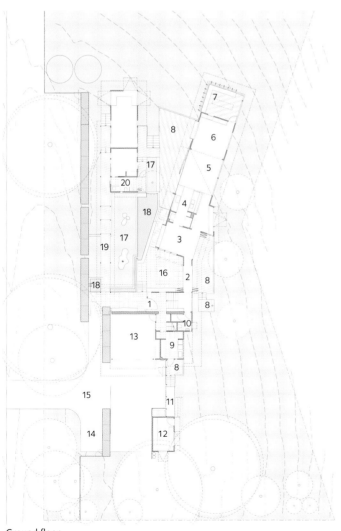

Ground floor

First floor

1 Entry
2 Hall
3 Dining area
4 Kitchen
5 Living area
6 Lounge
7 Covered deck
8 Deck
9 Laundry/utility room
10 Powder room
11 Drying area
12 Workshop
13 Carport
14 Visitor parking
15 Driveway
16 Covered terrace
17 Garden
18 Pond
19 Covered walkway
20 Bathroom
21 Master bedroom
22 Walk-in wardrobe
23 Master ensuite
24 Bedroom
25 Ensuite
26 Media lounge
27 Balcony

0   5m

Harbour House

Helliwell + Smith • Blue Sky Architecture Inc
West Vancouver, British Columbia, Canada

Given an almost impossible but spectacular site – a solid granite cliff overlooking Eagle Harbour – the house was formed as a continuation of the natural topographic lines, resulting in a series of dynamic curves and flying roofs sweeping across the rock face.

Particular attention was paid to the low-rise curving roof forms to help reduce the visual scale of the house, minimise the overall building height, and help open the house to natural light and the views over Eagle Harbour. The split-level planning helps accommodate the vertical circulation throughout the home. The house form steps back from the road as it rises up the cliffside.

The palette of materials chosen for the building is natural, durable and – as much as feasible – local. Exterior walls and fascias are constructed from clear natural red cedar siding, fibre cement siding, and glass.

The retaining walls for the driveway, entrance stairs and the foundation are fabricated from granite at the site and architectural concrete.

The partially covered terrace allows for outdoor living in all weather conditions; large overhangs protect the building from rain and sun. The house has a nautical feel in some of the detailing, and the curving cedar walls recall wooden boat hulls. The design of the home builds on the tradition of West Coast Modernism, creating a living environment inspired by and appreciative of the dramatic landscape of which it is a part.

Photography: Gillean Proctor

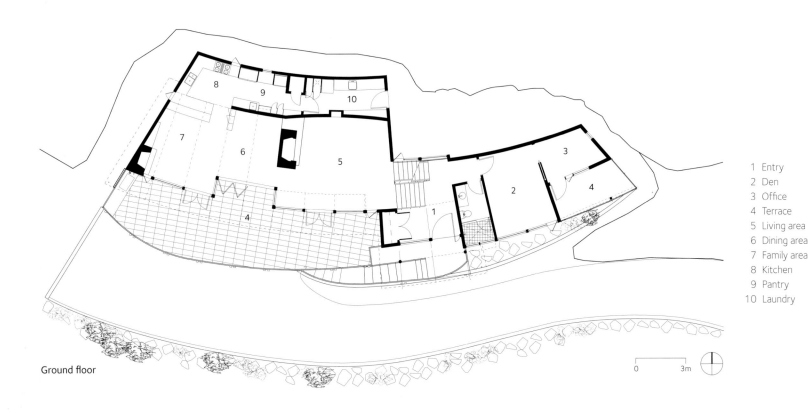

Ground floor

1 Entry
2 Den
3 Office
4 Terrace
5 Living area
6 Dining area
7 Family area
8 Kitchen
9 Pantry
10 Laundry

0   3m

Haus P

Caramel Architekten
Klosterneuburg, Lower Austria

Like a curious animal that might have been formed from Tetris blocks, Haus P seems to gaze down at the valley from its perch on this sloping property in Klosterneuburg. The seamless impression of the homogeneous sculptural form is strengthened by the use of prefabricated concrete elements in the façade. The access way on the street side follows the structure's longitudinal axis, passing the garage and terrace and entering the house, where it pushes past the dining room/kitchen area, cloakroom and stairway landing, and finally disappears out of the glazed front of the living room and into a breathtaking view of the Danubian plains.

The length of the building is interrupted only by the transverse orientation of the pool, which extends as a visual continuation of the lower covered terrace. Here at the lower, garden-access level there are two bedrooms, two bathrooms, a sauna, and a small studio

that opens out on the garden and the lower covered terrace. Located across from the studio on the other side of the terrace is the cellar, which is inserted into the slope beneath the garage.

Depending on its orientation, the façade is open or hermetic. While the west side with the dining room/ kitchen and terrace opens out fully onto the pool and garden, the east side, which faces the nearby neighbours, is almost completely closed off. Here, gill-like flaps direct the view towards the valley and create a private sphere for the living areas. By contrast, half the façade on the north side of the living area is thrown open, affording a complete view of the valley. This wide-open impression is intensified by the flush-glazed façade that extends overhead, becoming part of the roof. Interior design was by Sabine Bovelino.

Photography: Hertha Hurnaus

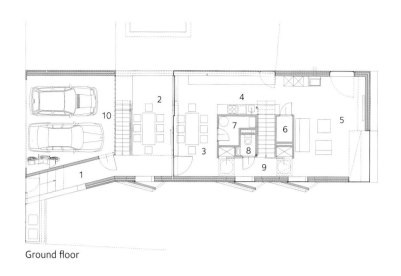

Ground floor

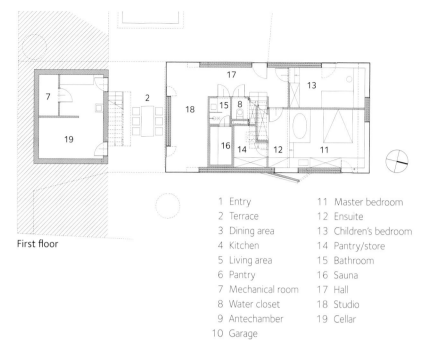

First floor

1 Entry
2 Terrace
3 Dining area
4 Kitchen
5 Living area
6 Pantry
7 Mechanical room
8 Water closet
9 Antechamber
10 Garage
11 Master bedroom
12 Ensuite
13 Children's bedroom
14 Pantry/store
15 Bathroom
16 Sauna
17 Hall
18 Studio
19 Cellar

133

Hawkesbury House

Marmol Radziner
Wanaka, New Zealand

Marmol Radziner served as design architect for this 200-square-metre (2150 square feet) three-bedroom home at the base of a windswept slope in the Wanaka Valley on the South Island of New Zealand. Herriot + Melhuish Architecture of Wellington co-ordinated the project locally as executive architect.

With distant views of alpine peaks, the 70-hectare (170 acres) hillside site overlooks rolling farmland. The site faces north, directly into the blazing sun of the southern hemisphere. Strict agency requirements limited both the size and form of the home in relation to the slope. The climate is one of extremes, with very hot summers and freezing cold winters.

The approach to building on this barren hillside was to merge with the slope, rather than to stick out from it. In response to the climactic extremes, a distinctive roof-form protects the home from the sun with generous roof overhangs. Inspired by the form of the hillside, the roof is shaped like an upside-down checkmark. A long,

thin footprint allows for views of the mountains from every room. Entry is through the side of the house with circulation along the back wall. Upon entering the rooms, the strong horizontals of the roof and deck frame the view.

The massing consists of two volumes – public and private – that are linked by a staircase. The first volume contains the 'great room' including the kitchen, living room and indoor/outdoor dining rooms. At the back of the great room, a wooden wall conceals the study, bathrooms, refrigerator and ladder access to a sleeping loft. Sliding glass doors open to the pool and exterior lounge area. A retaining wall, constructed of local stone known as Gibbston Valley Schist, runs from the living room to the exterior patio and incorporates an outdoor fireplace and benches. The second volume is the private wing containing the master bedroom and children's rooms.

Photography: Emily Andrews

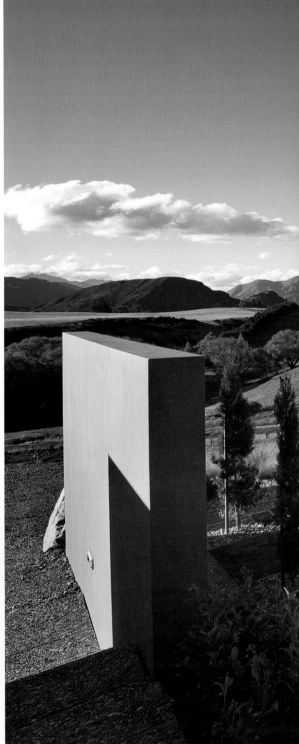

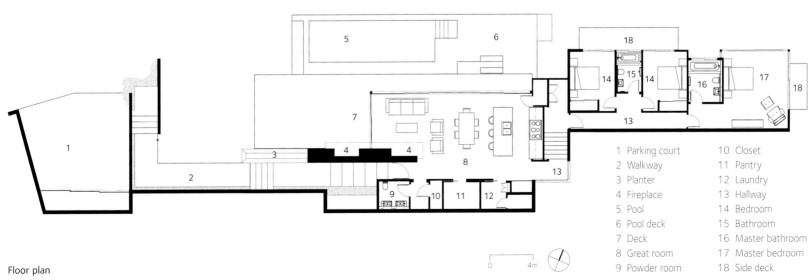

Floor plan

1 Parking court	10 Closet
2 Walkway	11 Pantry
3 Planter	12 Laundry
4 Fireplace	13 Hallway
5 Pool	14 Bedroom
6 Pool deck	15 Bathroom
7 Deck	16 Master bathroom
8 Great room	17 Master bedroom
9 Powder room	18 Side deck

0   4m

Hawthorn House

Richard Swansson Architect
Melbourne, Victoria, Australia

This project evolved over a number of years into the total redevelopment of a 19th-century villa and estate garden in suburban Melbourne. Developed during the decade-long drought that affected Melbourne in the first years of this century, the starting point was the replacement of the twee, water-hungry mock-Victorian garden with a contemporary garden whose design principles acknowledged the great garden designer of the Victorian era – William Guilfoyle – and most importantly required little water.

Hence the project developed water-harvesting and retention systems with an eclectic mix of botanical plantings laid out in picturesque style. The outbuildings developed as follies in the new landscape. The original buildings were restored, 1970's additions were taken out and the driveway moved from the middle of the site. This strategy allowed contemporary forms to sit beside the old. The interiors are similarly eclectic, reinterpreting the Victorian love of rich materials, overblown finishes and differently themed rooms.

The plan reflects the importance of zoning in a large family house and the fact the owner of the estate has to cook and do the dishes. It embodies passive solar principles and uses no town water. The living room faces onto the garden in the west; the cane screens solve the problem of the afternoon and evening sun. The house boasts a huge range of spatial experiences – every area was thought through by the architect and resolved with the owners.

Photography: Leah Robertson

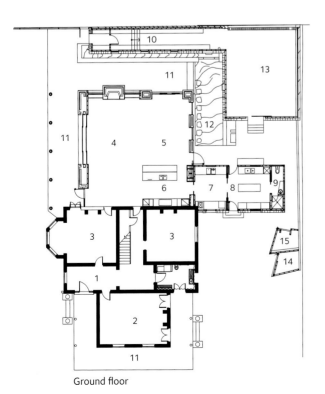

Ground floor

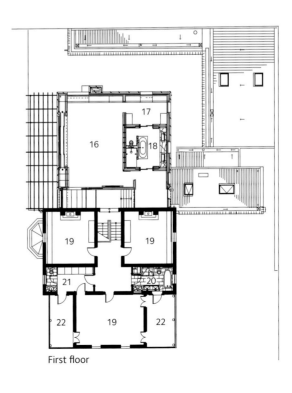

First floor

1 Entry
2 Sitting room
3 Study
4 Living area
5 Dining area
6 Kitchen
7 Pantry
8 Laundry
9 Powder room
10 Store
11 Terrace
12 Pond
13 Garage
14 Kennel
15 Pumps
16 Master bedroom
17 Master walk-in wardrobe
18 Master ensuite
19 Bedroom
20 Bathroom
21 Closet
22 Verandah

0   4m

Hollywood Hills Residence

Griffin Enright Architects
Los Angeles, California, USA

This 180-square-metre (2000 square feet) residence is located in a densely populated urban neighbourhood above Sunset Boulevard, where residents enjoy walking to local entertainment venues. The residence has views over Hollywood and out to the Pacific Ocean. Through relatively simple interventions, the architect was able to effect a complete transformation of the existing house. By removing only four interior walls on the ground floor, relocating a staircase, and adding two rooms stacked on top of each other, the interior was extended to create an open living space.

Additionally, natural light and views were enhanced to maximise the apparent volume of space, blurring the relationship between interior and exterior and connecting the front and rear yards. The intervention of two over-sized window boxes creates a new front façade, while providing a dramatic extension of the master bedroom suite and views of Los Angeles and beyond. The window boxes cantilever over a new front courtyard behind an existing garden wall and create an overhang for the new entry.

An existing staircase was relocated from the centre of the house to the area of the new two-storey addition, allowing new visual connections among the living, dining, kitchen and library spaces on the ground floor. The staircase ascends a half-flight through the stepped-up library to a landing connected to the backyard, and then switches back to arrive at an upper, sky-lit landing between the bedrooms above. The stair becomes a new central element connecting the stepped spatial volumes of the residence to the site, while simultaneously acting as an internal vertical courtyard that brings natural light and ventilation into the centre of the house.

The library contains an eye-level corner window at the ground level of the backyard and provides a new visual extension at the rear of the site. An elegant palette of minimal black and white materials serves to enhance the illusion of open and expansive space. The library is a room within a room – an effect that is enhanced by a material inversion; the living room has an ebony, fired-oak floor and a white ceiling, while the stepped-up library has a white epoxy resin floor with an ebony oak ceiling. The contrasting palette creates an interlocking condition which yields an apparent expansion of the space.

Photography: Benny Chan, Fotoworks

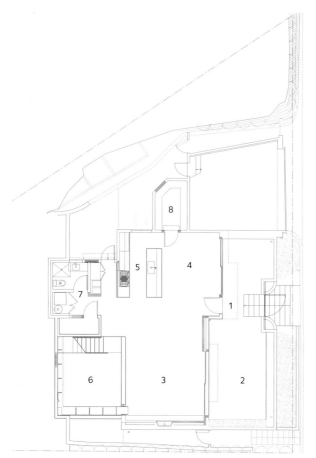

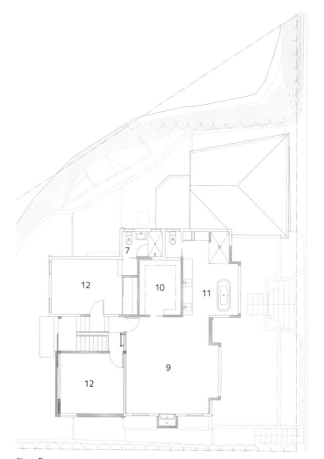

Ground floor

First floor

1 Entry
2 Courtyard
3 Living area
4 Dining area
5 Kitchen
6 Library
7 Shower room/water closet
8 Wine room
9 Master bedroom
10 Master walk-in wardrobe
11 Master ensuite
12 Bedroom
■ Rebuilt

0   2m

House 20 | Jolson
Melbourne, Victoria, Australia

Designed for 'empty nesters', this house met the client's brief that required each space within to be responsive to daily living while fulfilling specific needs. The parameters of a sheltered entry experience within a concrete home guided the evolution of the form. House 20 is space inhabited between plane, void and axis.

Jostling blades cantilever over a bronzed wall. A grassy mound below rises from the earth and creates arcing shelter and retreat. Beyond the spanning bronzed threshold, the interior is revealed as flowing space, sightlines penetrating deep within. A glazed void penetrates the plan – a room within a room – drawing in the natural environment. At its base, water mirrors the sky. Light and vision are moderated through woven mesh, which veils the void as if a lantern. The ground-plane opens up to the north through staggered mass walls.

Jolson's work explores form, which is anti-precedent and resides in the junction between sculpture and built form. This is guided by restraint and paring back of those decorative gestures that otherwise detract from the desire to frame and enhance space, and conceal complexity. Sophisticated simplicity informed the detailing and mechanics of the home – services being concealed or integrated within the architecture and interiors, or otherwise disappearing completely.

The design draws its strength by a continual dialogue between carefully articulated spaces, natural light and shadow, and unveiling of vertical and horizontal volumes. The brutal exterior penetrates the interior and become the foundation on which luxurious fabrics, textiles, furniture and lighting are juxtaposed.

Photography: Peter Bennetts

144

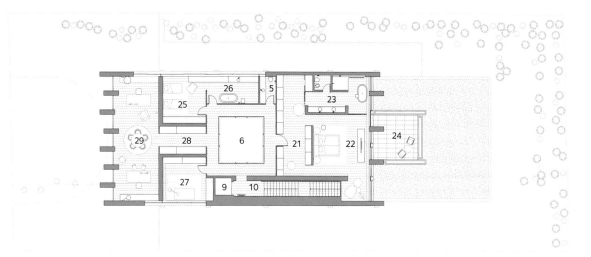

First floor

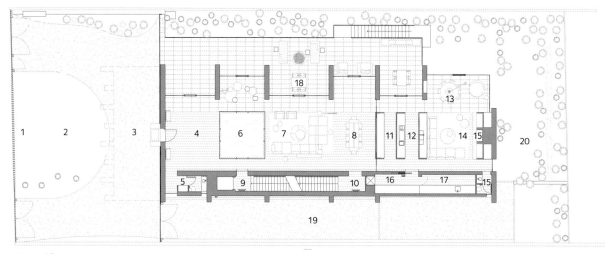

Ground floor

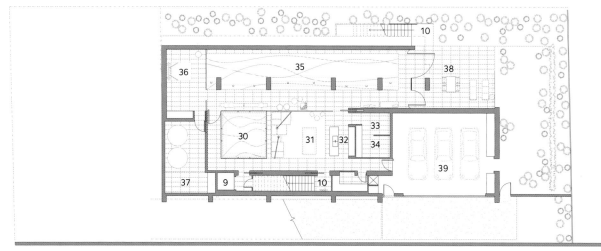

Basement

1   Aluminium fence
2   Landscape mound
3   Porte cochère
4   Entry hall
5   Powder room
6   Internal courtyard
7   Living area
8   Dining area
9   Lift
10 Staircase
11 Bar/pantry
12 Kitchen
13 Informal dining area
14 Family room
15 Fireplace
16 Scullery
17 Laundry
18 North terrace/loggia
19 Driveway
20 Rear garden
21 Master walk-in wardrobe
22 Master bedroom
23 Master ensuite
24 Private terrace
25 Bedroom
26 Ensuite
27 Guest bedroom
28 Library
29 Study
30 Water feature
31 Games room
32 Bar/kitchenette
33 Shower
34 Steam room
35 Indoor pool
36 Gym
37 Services
38 Loggia
39 Garage

0   4m

House Clifton Hill

Wilson & Hill Architects
Christchurch, New Zealand

The architect was commissioned to undertake this House on a cliff-top site in Christchurch that overlooks Sumner Beach and the mouth of the estuary, with panoramic views from Scarborough Heads around to the Southern Alps. The client provided a written brief that not only described the spaces required but also the 'feel' of the house for those living there and for guests. The brief stated the house should be calm, with beautiful views – sophisticated yet relaxed.

The house is built over three levels: the top level being the entry, the middle level containing garaging and bedrooms, with the lower (ground) level containing the living spaces and a guest bedroom. The orientation of the house and the positioning of the rooms ensures that each living space and bedroom has a view out over Pegasus Bay or Christchurch. The stone panels that clad the house give it a feeling of solidity, permanence and a strong connection with the ground, with living spaces opening directly onto stone terraces and flat lawns.

One of the challenging aspects of the design was how to bring people from the street at the rear of the site to the cliff edge at the front of the site so they experienced the full effect of the spectacular views. This has been achieved through the design of a journey starting with a level 'bridge' crossing the gap between the street edge and the entry of the house. Once inside the house, the visitor descends down the site through a three-level gallery space to the living areas stretched out along the cliff top. A timber deck provides the final step out to the cliff edge.

The gallery provides the circulation and ordering spine for the range of formal and informal spaces that connect to it and fulfils the client's request for a space to display his extensive art collection. The bedrooms, living areas and swimming pool with pool house are placed at right angles to the gallery, creating sheltered lawned courtyards and terraces on either side of the house. The master bedroom balcony offers dramatic views directly down to the base of the cliff some 50 metres (165 feet) below.

Photography: Stephen Goodenough

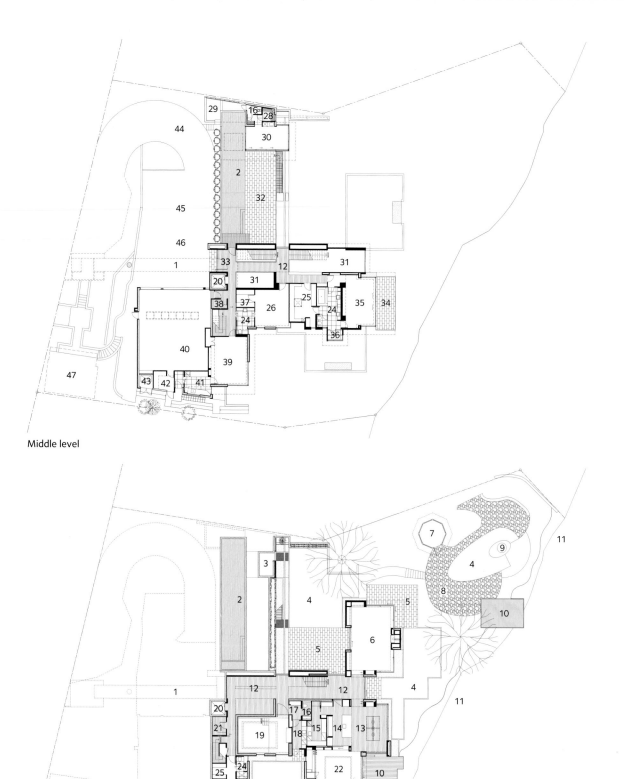

Middle level

Lower ground level

1 Entry bridge
2 Pool
3 Pond plant/store
4 Lawn
5 Terrace
6 Living
7 Turret
8 Paving
9 Sculpture
10 Deck
11 Cliff
12 Gallery
13 Dining
14 Kitchen
15 Scullery
16 Water closet
17 Cloakroom
18 Laundry
19 Home cinema
20 Lift
21 Wine store
22 Snug
23 Garden
24 Ensuite
25 Dressing room
26 Bedroom
27 Outdoor bath
28 Steam shower
29 Pool plant
30 Gym/pavilion
31 Void
32 Pool terrace
33 Middle level entry
34 Balcony
35 Master bedroom
36 Shower
37 Wardrobe
38 Store
39 Guest living room
40 Garage
41 Guest kitchen
42 Tool shed
43 Plant
44 Driveway
45 Parking
46 Forecourt
47 Existing cottage

0   5m

House Haller

Haller Jürgen & Peter Plattner
Mellau, Austria

The vision for this house was a customised building incorporating the impressive panorama at the foot of the Alps with a lifestyle demanding various solutions. The owners' specifications were a house combining living and working areas under one roof.

The entire design of this rather compact house conforms to the location and it was built into the slight incline of the land. As the hill-side of the house is embedded, the east-facing cellar area could be illuminated naturally and used as an office. There is direct access to the office via covered outdoor steps between the main entrance and the carport. Due to its positioning, the building catches the rays of the mountain sun in optimum fashion.

Despite being highly original and chunky to the point of appearing fortified, the building does not appear out of place in its surroundings. The mid-19th century heritage-protected Bregenzerwald farmhouse nearby is subtly reflected in the windows of the House Haller. Local tradition has been reinterpreted, focussing on aesthetic details without cutting back on functional aspects.

The entrance area is generous and includes a guest cloakroom. It is also possible to enter the house or the office from the double-space carport. The central staircase divides the ground floor into a living area and a kitchen/dining room. The bedrooms and an extra bathroom for guests are situated on the first floor. The master bathroom has a separate deck, which is ideal for relaxing and enjoying the magnificent views. The ridge and pitch of the roof give each first-floor room an individual character.

The internal walls and ceilings are covered with local silver fir wood, which gives the rooms a cosy feeling despite the large glass windows. The outside façade and the roof have been finished with local silver fir shingles. Here we can see how the architect has made use of a single material, testing its possibilities and constraints. What was once considered confined to traditional buildings appears here as experimental.

Photography: Albrecht Schnabel

Basement

Ground floor

First floor

1 Covered entry
2 Entry/cloakroom
3 Living room
4 Kitchen/dining room
5 Pantry
6 Covered sitting room
7 Deck
8 Well
9 Herb garden
10 Carport
11 Stainless mesh skylight
12 Master bedroom
13 Walk-in wardrobe
14 Master bathroom
15 Children's bedroom
16 Children's bathroom
17 Bedroom
18 Corridor
19 Office
20 Store/computer room
21 Water closet/shower
22 Studio
23 Store
24 Cellar
25 Archive
26 Covered office entry
27 Skylight

0   3m

House in Camps Bay

Luis Mira Architects
Cape Town, South Africa

The house is used as a holiday home by a single person, who often invites guest to stay. It needed to be a space that could be used as an open–plan studio, as well as being able to transform into private and individual spaces when the house is full of visitors. The privileged position of the land and the generous climate of Cape Town informed the design process: the client's brief required all rooms of the house to have a sea view.

The house focuses on the 'geographical room' of Camps Bay, the Atlantic Ocean, with the Lion's Head and Table Mountain in the backdrop. The design intention is applied by framing views towards the sea in the rooms, and opening up the terraces to look up at the mountains. The concept rests on creating a subtle journey through the open spaces and the interior that constantly glimpses at the landscape and merges with the architecture, and never reveals the entire building in a single instant.

In order to allow all rooms on the front of the house proximity to the sea, and to bring fresh air, light and circulation into the back of the house, two glass walled courtyards were introduced on the ground floor. One courtyard, built around the passage, connects the bedrooms; the other is built inside the main bedroom as part of the ensuite area. Both courtyards offer sea views.

The use of neutral and natural materials is a response to the desire to bring the outdoors inside, achieved by contrasting the exuberant landscape with the 'blank canvas' of the interior. This situation is enabled by 'peeling off' the volume of the interior spaces towards the north – the source of sunlight in the southern hemisphere. The ultimate concept of luxury is the constant extending and opening of the inside spaces to meet in full the unique and exquisite South African climate.

Photography: Wieland Gleich and Mira Architects

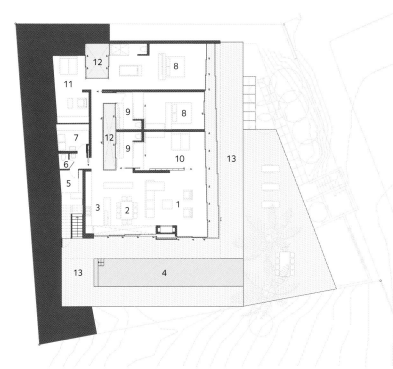

Ground floor

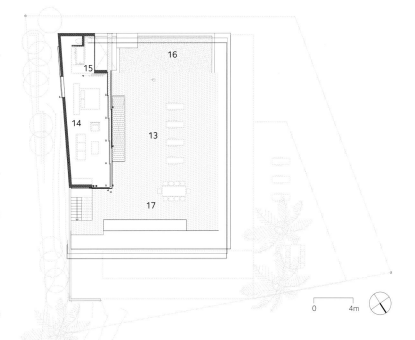

First floor

1 Lounge	7 Laundry	13 Deck
2 Dining area	8 Bedroom	14 Bedroom/gym
3 Kitchen	9 Ensuite	15 Ensuite
4 Pool	10 Study/bedroom	16 Roof garden
5 Changing room	11 Dressing room	17 Outdoor dining area
6 Water closet	12 Courtyard	

0   4m

House in Txai Itacaré

Saraiva + Associados
Itacaré, Bahia State, Brazil

The setting for this house in Bahia is tropical – a mixture of heavy rains and intense sun. It offers a dramatic and exotic landscape, and indeed the first field visit the architect took with the owner was during a tropical downpour. Parallel to the ocean, near the sandy beach, above a canopy of coconut palms, the residential complex sits atop the steep slope of a hill, overlooking the Atlantic.

The architect's brief was to accommodate a 400-square-metre (4300 square feet) house within a 1800-square-metre (19,375 square feet) site that offers a magnificent sea view. The house had to have independent access, while allowing for the option of a second residence to be built in the future. An extensive platform preserved a wide part of the natural scenery – linear and slender, yet predominantly terrestrial, it is volume that works as a social and leisure core. In fact, this linear quality responded perfectly to the wishes of the owner. The bedrooms

sit at the northern and southern extremities, offering a wide perspective to the ocean. They are interconnected through open and wooded suspended walkways.

As a beach house, informality reigns and informed most architectural decisions. Its language and tone is neutral in order to fit in with the local flora and population. Materials are simple but of exceptional quality – certified and sourced from the local environment. Furthermore, they remain as bold and natural as possible, without undergoing major alteration. For instance, Brazilian teak is sawn and used in its rough state by presenting the natural cutting texture. Also sourced from Bahia state, the marble is unpolished, almost coarse. The lighting in this house is largely dependent on the rays of the sun and offers an understated ambiance. The simple, neutral exterior is completed by ceramic white tiles on the roof.

Photography: Images kindly supplied by the owner

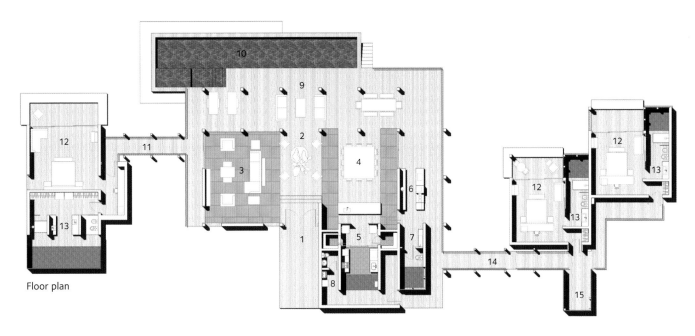

Floor plan

1 Entry hall
2 Living area
3 Television area
4 Dining area
5 Kitchen
6 Barbecue
7 Pool water closet
8 Utility room/water closet
9 Verandah
10 Pool
11 North walkway
12 Bedroom
13 Ensuite
14 South walkway
15 Stairwell

0   4m

house R

The house is located in the Stadtgarten (city park) in the centre of Karlsruhe. The property was once part of a villa. A pavilion that belongs to the historic ensemble forms part of the wall that encloses the property on three sides. The four-storey single family house is reached via a forecourt and a ramp; the main entrance on the northern side and a second entrance via the carport lead to the entrance area.

The storeys are connected by an open stairway and a lift, which facilitates use by the elderly and disabled. On the ground floor are the entrance area, home office, double-height living room and kitchen and dining area. The first floor houses a gallery that serves as a more intimate living area, two children's rooms, a dressing room and two bathrooms. The attic floor, which has a roof terrace on three sides, is reserved for the parents. It is not divided into rooms; instead the individual functional devices – bed, wash basin, bath tub, water closet, shower stall and dressing area – are arranged in a loft-style layout.

In the basement is a swimming pool with a projecting skylight, guest room, bathroom and mechanical room. In order to achieve optimal exposure to light in the basement, the ground floor floats 1 metre (3 feet) above the terrain level, in order to create a window-band 50 centimetres high (20 inches). The window-band and skylight flood the basement with natural light.

Cross-ventilation occurs automatically by controlled louvre windows. The glass areas are equipped with exterior sun protection that screens the residents from public view at the same time. Thanks to night cooling and exterior sun-protection, it was not necessary to install air-conditioning. The thermal mass of the concrete walls functions as a store of cool air and cools rooms throughout the day. By using triple-glazed windows, highly effective insulation and a solar thermal system, an energy-optimised building has been realised.

Photography: Thomas Herrmann

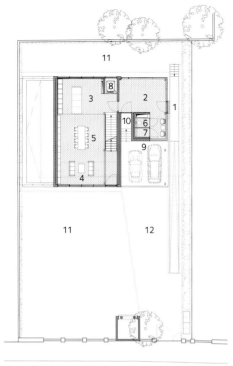

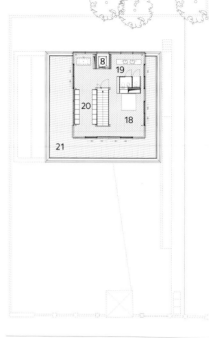

Ground floor

First floor

Attic floor

1 Main entry
2 Office
3 Kitchen
4 Living area
5 Dining area
6 Bathroom
7 Cloakroom
8 Lift
9 Carport
10 Entry from carport
11 Garden
12 Driveway
13 Gallery
14 Children's room
15 Bathroom
16 Dressing room
17 Void
18 Master bedroom
19 Master ensuite
20 Master dressing room
21 Roof terrace

House with ZERO stairs

100% Przemek Kaczkowski & Ola Targonska
Wrocław, Poland

The clients, a middle-aged couple, approached the architect with a specific request: they wanted to build a house with no stairs that would be practical and enjoyable in their old age. The site was in suburban Wrocław among disappearing traces of a rural past, surrounded by houses of all styles. The volume of the house shelters the remaining large garden from unwanted views and noise.

The T-shaped plan reflects the distribution of uses within the house. The long wing visible from the street accommodates the common spaces of the house, while the almost entirely solid front façade, clad with wooden slats, forms the closed backside of the large living area.

On entering the house through a wooden door one sees the other face of the house – its long, glazed façade opening to the sunny terrace and the garden. The terrace is clad with light-coloured terrazzo in large tiles and is connected to the garden by a wide ramp with strips of grass and grey granite paving blocks.

The central entrance point allows for convenient and discreet communication to both wings of the house. The 'public' wing features a slanted ceiling, adding to the feeling of openness and spaciousness. Behind the side wall of the living room, connected by a two-sided fireplace, is a home cinema space with acoustically-clad walls and an incorporated screen.

The kitchen is at the heart of the plan and is a transition space between the living room and the bedroom wing. The three bedrooms also open to the terrace and the garden with full-height sliding windows. A narrow strip of water runs outside, ensuring privacy. The row of bedrooms features a bathroom at each end, and the corridor is lit by square skylights.

Photography: Sebastian Oleksik

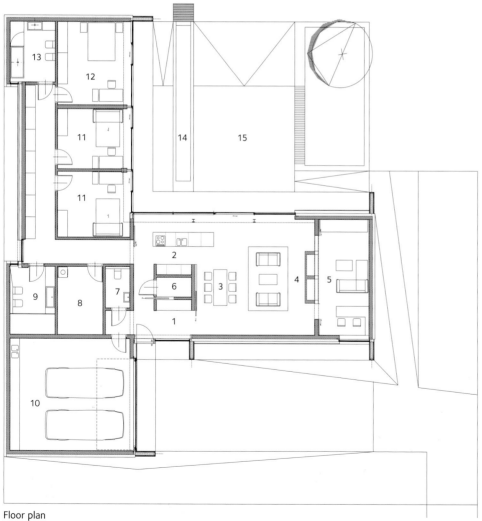

1 Entry
2 Kitchen
3 Dining area
4 Living area
5 Video room
6 Store
7 Water closet
8 Technical room
9 Bathroom
10 Garage
11 Bedroom
12 Master bedroom
13 Bathroom
14 Water feature
15 Terrace

Floor plan

0   3m

Infiniski Casa Manifesto

Infiniski by James & Mau Architects
Curacaví, Chile

This house embodies bioclimatic design, the use of recycled materials, non-polluting constructive systems and integration of renewable energy. The project relies on bioclimatic architecture adapting the form and positioning of the house to its energy needs. The project is based on a prefabricated and modular design allowing a cheaper and faster means of construction. This modular system also allows future modifications or enlargements in order to adapt easily to the evolving needs of the client.

The house is divided into two levels and uses three recycled maritime containers as structure. A container cut in two parts on the first level is used as the support structure for the containers on the second level. This structure in the form of a bridge creates an extra space between the containers, isolated with thermal glass panels. As a consequence, with only 90 square metres (970 square feet) of container floor, the project generates a total of 160 square metres (1720 square feet), reducing significantly the use of extra building materials.

This structure in the form of a bridge responds to the bioclimatic needs of the house. Form follows energy, and offers an effective natural ventilation system. It also helps to take full advantage of the house's natural surroundings, natural light and landscape views.

As if it had a second skin, the house 'dresses and undresses' itself, thanks to ventilated external solar covers on walls and roof, that supply natural solar heating. The house uses two types of covers or 'skin': wooden panels sourced from sustainable forests on one side and recycled mobile pallets on the other.

The pallets can be opened in winter to allow the sun to heat the metal surface of the container walls, and close in summer to protect the house from the heat. This skin also serves as an exterior aesthetic finish, helping the house to better integrate into its environment.

Both exterior and interior use up to 85 per cent recycled, reused and eco-friendly materials: recycled cellulose and cork for insulation, recycled aluminium, iron and wood, noble wood from sustainable forests, ecological paint and eco-label ceramics. Thanks to its bioclimatic design and the installation of alternative energy systems, the house achieves 70 per cent energy autonomy.

Photography: Antonio Corcuera

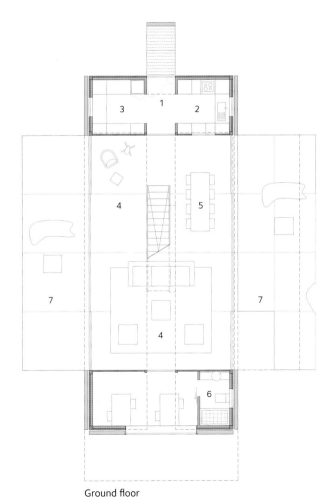

Ground floor

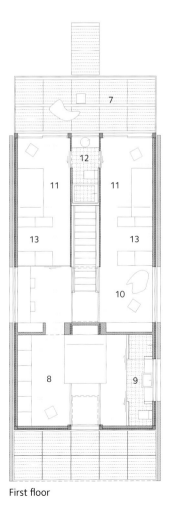

First floor

1 Entry
2 Kitchen
3 Laundry
4 Living area
5 Dining area
6 Bathroom
7 Terrace
8 Master bedroom
9 Master ensuite
10 Studio
11 Bedroom
12 Ensuite
13 Walk-in wardrobe

0   2m

Isola di Albarella Villa

Gabbiani&Associati
Isola di Albarella, Rovigo, Italy

The villa sits on the private island of Albarella, off the north-east coast of Italy in the Adriatic. Water and sky were the project's two driving elements, with the ground acting as a subtle interface line. Continuity between the house, the garden and the greater landscape is achieved through broad windows that intersect the floors, extending uninterrupted to the swimming pool, which unites the private space with the broad horizon of the lagoon.

The subdivision of the villa into three simple, distinct but interconnected volumes, all faced in a copper mantle with supple lines, harmonises with the prospects onto the water and the direction of the prevailing winds. In the interior, the bathrooms are finished in blue and green glass mosaics featuring stylised motifs, evoking the flora and fauna of the lagoon. These provide the colour accent to the house, which otherwise features wood, natural metal and white tones.

Given that the primary view from the house is over the water and sandbanks, a curved, panelled wooden roof was designed to integrate harmoniously into the landscape and helps to reduce the volumetric appearance of the building. It recalls the natural sand dunes of the Adriatic coast and a boat anchored on the lagoon shore.

Photography: Arnaldo Dal Bosco, Marcella Gabbiani

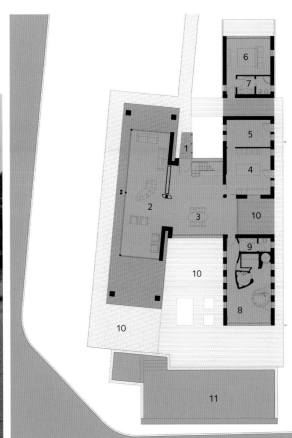

1 Entry
2 Living room
3 Dining area
4 Kitchen
5 Pantry
6 Bedroom
7 Ensuite
8 Spa/shower
9 Powder room
10 Deck
11 Pool

Ground floor

John Chapman Residence

Bowen Architecture
Sarasota, Florida, USA

Modest in size and finish, the focus of John Chapman Residence is on ease of living. John's reputation for hosting social events is notable. His spacious property is conducive to large gatherings by virtue of its size and central city location. John asked for a modestly priced home that might work for a future family but for the meantime, it should be low-maintenance with a landscape to match. The architect took for granted that it must also be a gathering place for large parties. Considering the Florida climate, this meant that the outdoor space must be the most important space. The architecture must be utilitarian, simple and supportive of the outdoor space.

The house is in a very simple shed-form, sheltered from the sun by nestling into existing mature oak trees along the southern property border. The plan opens onto a continuous porch that overlooks the main garden space which contains an outdoor bar, swimming pool and spa. The area adjacent to the main garden is planned for a sand volleyball court. An open carport is connected to the porch roof and cantilevers over the main entry gate. A shell entry court and constructed sand dune create a minimalist foreground for a simple home.

The main material is corrugated 'galvalume' metal siding and roofing, giving this home its nickname: the Metal House. The exposed structure is galvanised steel. The porch and carport ceilings are clad with unfinished cement board. Doors and windows are clear anodised aluminium. The interior features burlap-cured concrete slab floors that resemble large slabs of limestone. Cabinetry is made from bamboo with recycled glass and coloured concrete surfaces. The site is sand, crushed shell, native dune grasses, coconut palms and existing mature oak trees.

The home sits on a busy local street located along the eastern edge of the property. This street relationship is buffered by a continuous metal wall set at the back of the entrance court, locating the home in relation to the environment rather than the street. With attention to basic ideas including site orientation, building shading and native landscape, the John Chapman Residence achieves an ecological sensibility through passive design.

Photography: George Cott

1 Porch
2 Living area
3 Kitchen
4 Dining area
5 Office
6 Powder room
7 Bedroom
8 Ensuite
9 Mechanical room and laundry
10 Master bedroom
11 Master ensuite
12 Master closet
13 Outdoor shower

Floor plan

0   3m

Johnson Residence

Obie G Bowman Architect
Healdsburg, California, USA

This 260-square-metre (2800 square feet) winter house for a retired couple from Washington State sits on 4 hectares (10 acres) of steeply sloped conifer and hardwood forest. The combination of gentle slope, northerly view and southerly sun occurs where the easterly edge of the forest gives way to a small clearing straddling the easterly property line. Winter sun exposure was carefully studied and strongly influenced the placement and forms of the house, with its main spaces affording northerly views while capturing sunlight through south-facing clerestories.

The clerestories sit atop a full-length feature-wall that includes pantry and storage areas, a window seat, cantilevered shelving and an art display. The rooms across the hall have interior clerestories of their own, allowing the light to continue into these spaces. Three partially roofed terraces extend the interior spaces to the outside, off the kitchen, bedroom, and living/dining area. Cantilevered roofs above the end-terraces slope up towards the south to receive low winter sun. Openings assure balanced light quality and visual contact with the conifer boughs above while providing enough solid surfaces to provide shade or protection from the rain.

The perpendicular utility wing of the house extends back into the hillside and includes a mechanical room, office, garage and an animal care room (the owners are noted animal welfare advocates). The entire wing is lit naturally by a continuous roof monitor. The main space structure comprises wide, painted steel flanges with Douglas fir beams and structural decking to mitigate potential damage from falling trees and branches. Other interior materials include maple doors, painted gypsum board walls and millwork. Exterior materials are primarily concrete and Galvalume sheet metal, selected for their fire-resistance and low-maintenance characteristics.

Photography: Obie G. Bowman

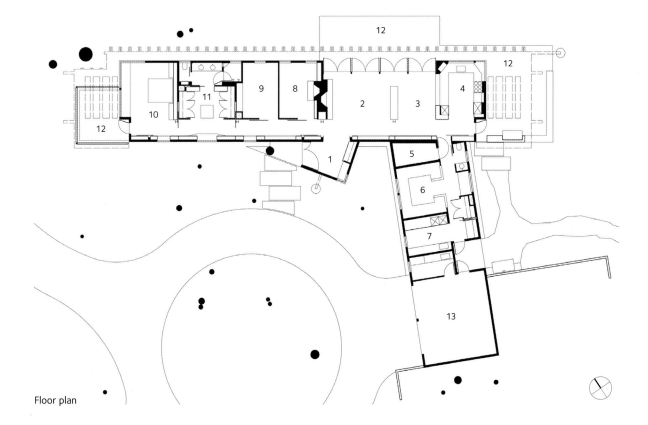

Floor plan

1 Entry
2 Living area
3 Dining area
4 Kitchen
5 Mechanical room
6 Office
7 Laundry
8 Den
9 Exercise room
10 Bedroom
11 Ensuite
12 Terrace
13 Garage

174

Kapoor House

Swatt | Miers Architects
Berkeley, California, USA

The Kapoor House has been designed to take full advantage of some of the most dramatic views in Northern California, including five bridges over San Francisco Bay. The site is the highest rock outcropping in the Berkeley hills, with precipitous slopes on the east, west and south sides. Because of the limited accessible site area due to steep slopes, it was decided that the architecture would need to create its own usable landscape. The motor court doubles as a courtyard for entertaining and leads to a series of stairs that culminate in a bridge hovering over a reflecting pool and a second entry courtyard that leads to the first floor entry.

The south and east sides of the home have been developed with dramatic cantilevered terraces for outdoor entertaining, and for enjoying uninterrupted Bay Area views from Mount Diablo to the Golden Gate Bridge. The interior relies on open-planning to expand space horizontally and vertically. Large pocket doors allow the entire kitchen and breakfast wing to be closed off as needed for entertaining, or opened to reveal a glazed corner, with pocketing glass doors on two walls that seamlessly dissolve the separation between interior and exterior space.

Detailing is crisp and simple and the materials – mainly Halila limestone, Honduran mahogany and kaya wood – are kept to a minimum, creating an environment that is both quiet and reserved, yet bold and dramatic at the same time. Complementing the simplicity of the interiors, special artistic details brought by the owners from their native India add richness to the composition.

Photography: Tim Griffith

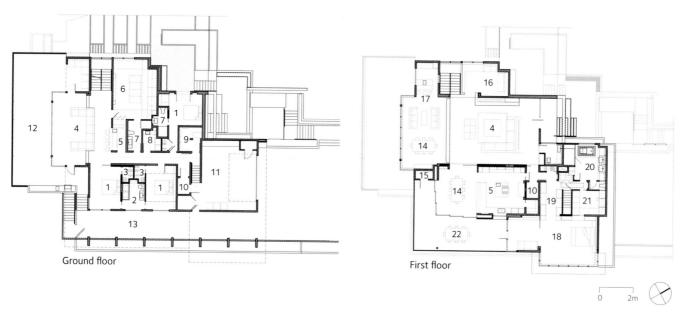

Ground floor

First floor

1 Bedroom
2 Ensuite
3 Walk-in wardrobe
4 Living area
5 Kitchen
6 Theatre
7 Powder room
8 Utility room
9 Mechanical room
10 Lift
11 Garage
12 Terrace
13 Breezeway
14 Dining area
15 Store
16 Library
17 Bar
18 Master bedroom
19 Master walk-in wardrobe
20 Master ensuite
21 Office
22 Deck

0   2m

Kooyong Residence

Matt Gibson Architecture + Design
Armadale, Victoria, Australia

The Kooyong Residence involved a renovation and restoration of a decrepit grand Victorian dwelling. After gentle persuasion from the architect, the client agreed to retain the front elements of the historical building. Following the removal of a previous extension, the extensive brief requested an upper-level addition, garage and pool, allowing greater interaction with the exterior.

The architect's choice (given the depth of the site) was to separate rather than attach the new works to the rear of the existing building, availing textured areas of external space between old and new 'pavilions'. Two levels of sculpted L-shaped floor area are stacked over each other at the rear, utilising the limits of the site. The soft and sinuous use of timber-cladding extends the low-energy theme and assists in enhancing a sculptural and organic point of difference to the rigidity and masculinity of the historical building.

Central and side courtyards provide important breezeways and powerful interstitial transition points within the site. A glazed covered way extending off the original hallway connects the buildings, providing

a metaphorical 'bridge' and a thermal regulator, with the flexibility to open the house up completely to the elements. The hallway continues as a main axis through the length of the site, setting up a series of framed scenes and a journey of discovery. At the rear, 70 solid recycled Blackbutt fins provide privacy from neighbouring houses and address solar emission concerns as they disperse gradually from east to north, breaking down a seemingly solid façade at one end to be completely permeable at the other.

As opposed to other dwellings within this suburban context in Melbourne, where important references to Victorian and wider Australian heritage may be obliterated without intervention, this project utilises and exploits the juxtaposition between traditional and modern to heighten and delight in the difference, while following sustainable methods that encourage retention and reuse rather than demolition.

Photography: Shannon McGrath

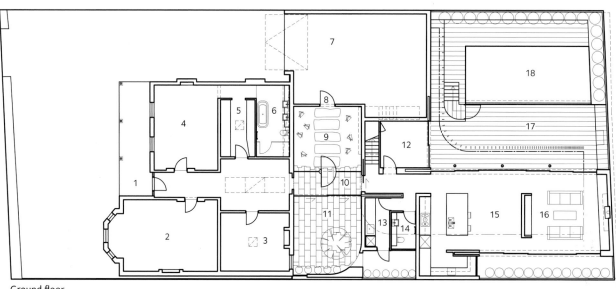

Ground floor

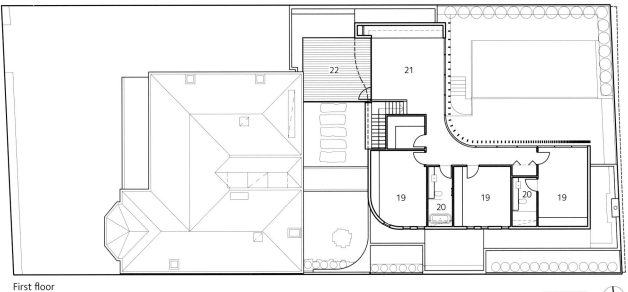

First floor

1 Front entry
2 Drawing room/library
3 Study/guest bedroom
4 Master bedroom
5 Walk-in wardrobe
6 Master ensuite
7 Garage
8 Side entry
9 Entry court
10 Prism
11 Central courtyard
12 Snug
13 Laundry
14 Water closet
15 Kitchen/dining area
16 Family room
17 External living area
18 Pool
19 Bedroom
20 Ensuite
21 Playroom
22 Roof deck

0   6m

Lake Forest Park Renovation

FINNE Architects
Near Seattle, Washington State, USA

Located on a secluded, wooded site about 40 kilometres (25 miles) miles north of Seattle, this 1950s house has been completely renovated while retaining the spirit of the original building. With extensive new windows and glazed roof monitors, the renovated house appears to be a glass pavilion in the forest. The floor plan has been reorganised to create a spacious, light-filled master bedroom and master bathroom, with each space surrounded by glass and views to the forest. The main living and dining spaces have been slightly enlarged, and a new roof monitor with high windows has been added to bring soft natural light to the entire space.

The new, enlarged kitchen has counters in quartz and cast glass, with continuous windows extending directly to the counter level. The existing hemlock ceiling with exposed fir beams in roughly half the house has been retained, and new fir ceilings have been added to the remainder. The existing terrazzo flooring has been refinished, with new areas of terrazzo added in a complementary colour.

Consistent with the original simplicity and clarity of the house, a palette of new materials has been added to create powerful juxtapositions of texture and colour, allowing each material to benefit from adjacent contrasting surfaces. Casework consists primarily of cherry panels: some are smooth while others have been milled to make a texture evocative of 'woven wood.' An accent wall about 10 metres long (30 feet) adjacent to the dining and kitchen areas has been clad entirely in weathered steel panels. Suspended casework on the steel wall utilises either resin panels with natural grasses or textured cherry wood, with both materials set against the variegated umber colours of the steel.

In keeping with other projects by FINNE Architects, this renovation has pursued the idea of 'crafted modernism,' the enrichment of a modernist aesthetic with highly personal crafted materials and objects. Custom fabrications include the cast-glass kitchen counter, steel wall panels, suspended steel mirror frames, laser-cut steel shade valences, custom steel lighting bars,

hand-blown glass light fixtures and a number of custom furniture pieces. The glass wall between the master bedroom and master bathroom has been transformed with the use of a hand-drawn pattern in etched glass, with the pattern becoming more dense at the bottom, for privacy, and increasingly transparent at the top.

Sustainable design practices were integral to the project from the start. Radiant heating under terrazzo flooring creates an even heat source with maximum energy efficiency. High clerestory windows bring natural light deep into the house and motorised operators allow for ventilation during the summer. Green materials including resin panels, quartz counters, linoleum, low VOC paint and sustainable wood products were used in the project. The intense craftsmanship and detailing of the renovation underlies a sustainable principle: build well and it will last for many years.

Photography: Benjamin Benschneider

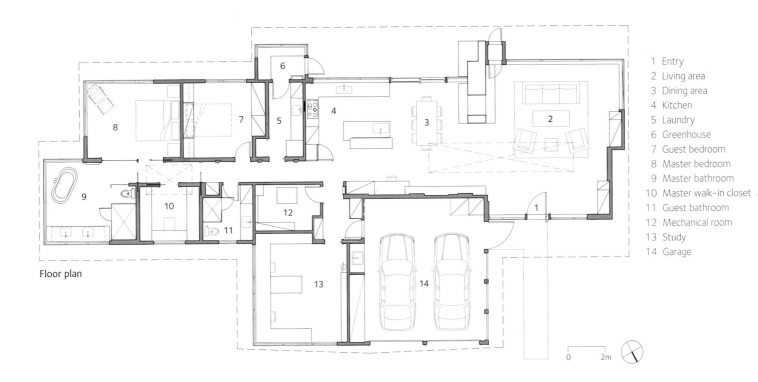

Floor plan

1 Entry
2 Living area
3 Dining area
4 Kitchen
5 Laundry
6 Greenhouse
7 Guest bedroom
8 Master bedroom
9 Master bathroom
10 Master walk-in closet
11 Guest bathroom
12 Mechanical room
13 Study
14 Garage

0   2m

Link House

Carol Kurth Architecture, PC
Westchester, New York, USA

Link House is a thoughtful renovation and addition to a modern, passive-solar home. Carol Kurth, FAIA was the designer of the original 1983 home and was recommissioned for the renovation and addition in 2010, which integrates the new owners' programmatic goals with contemporary materials and technologies.

An early proponent of sustainable architecture, Kurth designed the original home to minimise site disturbance, provide a natural and maintenance-free setting, maximise daylight and create views into the surrounding woods, enable natural ventilation, and accommodate a passive solar heating and hot water system – a new technology at the time. An innovative feature of the home was the two-storey passive solar wall with calculated overhangs, which maintained a consistent indoor environment, allowing sunlight in the winter months and providing shade in the summer.

The original client's desire for casual family space included a loft-style living space with a flowing 'great room', a ground-floor master suite, and an upper-level guest suite.

Five owners and 25 years later, the architect was contacted by the current owners to update and expand the home. The new programme includes a second-level music pavilion, an additional guest suite with bath, modifications to the master suite, the addition of three roof terraces, restoration of the exterior facade, and a new pool amenity. A new glass 'link' was designed to bridge existing and new spaces, while volumetric forms replicate elements from the 1983 design: overlapping volumes, curved and truncated corners, 'pipe' railings and glass block windows. Clerestory windows admit soft natural sunlight and transform the music library into a brightly-lit, tree-top pavilion.

Interior elements include limestone countertops in spa-like hues of whites and creams that are complemented by custom-designed, cedar plank wall-paneling. A new linear fireplace separates the two main double-height spaces and energy-efficient mechanical systems were completely upgraded. Exterior façades were re-clad with low-maintenance cedar siding and renewed landscaping features include preserving the natural ground covers and indigenous plantings to keep the site 'mow-free'. The dramatic outdoor backdrop and swimming pool were designed in collaboration with Benedek & Ticehurst Landscape Architects. A gridded 'green' wall to cultivate clematis was installed, and photovoltaic roof panels are planned. The revitalisation updates this classically modern home into a sustainable modernist composition for the 21st century.

Photography: Albert Vecerka/ESTO, Peter Krupenye (p.189)

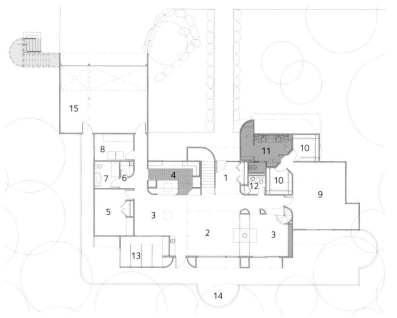

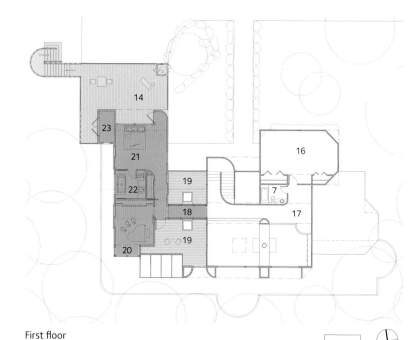

Ground floor

First floor

0 8m

- ▓ Restoration/Addition 2010
- ☐ Original 1983

1 Entry	7 Bathroom
2 Great room	8 Laundry
3 Dining area	9 Master bedroom
4 Kitchen	10 Walk-in closet
5 Office	11 Master bathroom
6 Pantry	12 Powder room

13 Greenhouse	19 Roof garden
14 Sun deck	20 Music room
15 Garage	21 Guest bedroom
16 Bedroom	22 Ensuite
17 Loft	23 Mechanical room/store
18 Link	

Longacres

Damien Murtagh Architects
Burrow Peninsula, Dublin, Ireland

This coastal dwelling in the Burrow Peninsula in the North County of Dublin lies on a sand and gravel ridge of salt marshes and dune grasslands that abound with flora and fauna throughout the year. It is among the most scenic and peaceful places anywhere in Ireland. The client's brief proposed that the form, scale and overall visual appearance of the house had to evolve from its rural and coastal environment setting.

The building consists of a two-storey elongated spine off which extend two additional arms at either end that together form a private sunny courtyard. The principal aim behind this form is to take full advantage of the extraordinary coastal views from most rooms in the house while capturing the sun's progress throughout the day. All the social spaces enjoy dual aspects so that the coastal panorama and sunlight are present.

An open-plan layout has been adopted within which voids, frameless glass railings and sliding walls allow playful interaction and communication throughout.

Externally dry stonewalls, brilliant white stucco rendering, patina copper and cedar cladding blend effortlessly together and into their surroundings. The result is a light-filled home where adults and children alike are in constant touch with the outside world while sheltered from the elements.

A recessed alcove set at the junction of the protective dry stonewall and white rendered elongated spinal core forms the main entrance to the house. Giant slabs of warm travertine stone set against the brilliant white internal walls, voids to the basement and first floor and large expanses of glazing create a striking light-filled entrance hall. The open-plan kitchen, dining and living areas are accessed through a large sliding door. Off the dining area is a raised living space, separated by a cantilevered staircase with frameless glass rail, encased in white corian.

Across a bridge that traverses the circulation core are three bedrooms, including the master bedroom, which has a sheltered morning terrace and a guest bedroom with its own roof terrace. The outcome of this design responds sensitively yet boldly to both its surroundings and requirements. The design, form and harmonious synthesis of materials is a modern interpretation of Celtic coastal architecture.

Photography: Michael Taylor, Anthony Hopkins

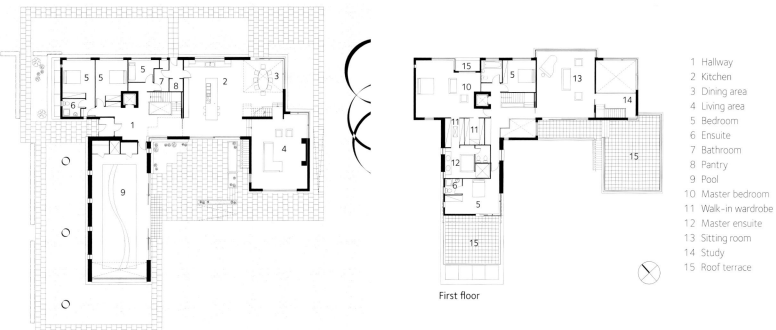

1	Hallway
2	Kitchen
3	Dining area
4	Living area
5	Bedroom
6	Ensuite
7	Bathroom
8	Pantry
9	Pool
10	Master bedroom
11	Walk-in wardrobe
12	Master ensuite
13	Sitting room
14	Study
15	Roof terrace

Ground floor

First floor

Mandeville Canyon Residence

Griffin Enright Architects
Brentwood, California, USA

The site for this project is on a cul-de-sac that creates a tapered lot manifesting in a small curved front yard lot line, while the rear yard of the site opens to the canyon and city views. Two distinct conditions emerge from the design: from the rear yard the house is seen as part of a series of horizontal volumes that merge with the terrain of the landscape, while the front yard presence of the house is distinctly more urban, vertical and formal. This dichotomy between the front and back zones of the property is emphasised by the articulation of two vertical walls that are folded into roof surfaces to create a backdrop that anchors the horizontal terrain.

The two shell-like walls shift in plan to differentiate a formal entry and construct specific views of the canyon beyond. This volumetric fissure creates a two-storey entry that contains the stair to the first-floor bedrooms. A large opening at the landing of the stair frames the first glimpse of the canyon beyond, while a larger opening leads to the living area and reveals the expansive vista overlooking the city beyond. The open-plan living, dining and kitchen areas are surrounded by moveable glass doors that telescope open to the elongated porch.

The exterior deck and landscape are merged with the topography, creating a lap pool along the site ledge and a stair to the landscape below. A slight shifting of the volumes from the ground floor to the first floor creates large covered exterior areas, and the first floor is bisected by an open court that separates the master bedroom from the children's bedrooms. The master bedroom is positioned at the cantilevered corner of the house to maximise views both up the canyon and to the city vista, while a covered deck area along the perimeter creates outdoor spaces connected to the terrain of the site.

Photography: Tim Street-Porter

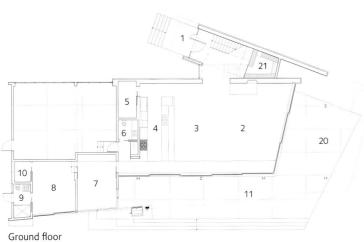

Ground floor

First floor

0   4m

1 Entry	8 Gym	15 Playroom
2 Living area	9 Shower room	16 Child's bedroom
3 Dining area	10 Closet	17 Child's ensuite
4 Kitchen	11 Terrace	18 Closet
5 Pantry	12 Master bedroom	19 Open deck
6 Powder room	13 Master ensuite	20 Covered deck
7 Library	14 Walk-in wardrobe	21 Wine room

Methven House

Swatt | Miers Architects
Marin County, California, USA

The Methven House is located on a steep east-facing hillside, dotted with beautiful heritage oak trees, in rural San Anselmo, and accessed by a long, narrow, serpentine road. A single magnificent giant oak dominates a clearing, deep into the 0.8 hectare (2 acre) site, where the house is located. Like threading a needle, the design twists and turns between tree canopies over five levels, so that all major spaces focus on the grand oak in the centre of the clearing, and open to exterior patios cut into the hill, or terraces that hover above.

The house is anchored to its site by two vertical cast-in-place concrete stair elements. A sky-lit stair tower, doubling as the entry at the north side of the house, leads to a private office and roof terrace at the lower-middle level, and terminates at split-level dining and living spaces at the upper-middle level. A second staircase, bordered by a single cast-in-place concrete wall, complements the entry stair tower as it anchors the east side of the house, and leads to the bedrooms

at the upper level. Along the north–south axis, a two-storey circulation spine overlooking the large central oak tree connects both stairs to the kitchen, family room, and terrace at the south side.

Interior spaces are minimally defined by level and material changes, and are visually connected horizontally and vertically to adjacent spaces. As an example, from the upper stair landing, one can simultaneously view the upper-level bridge, the two-storey dining space, the mid-level two-storey circulation spine and the living room.

The use of natural materials, such as quarter-sawn red oak floors, Afromosia casework and built-in seating, exposed Douglas fir glue-laminated beams and decking, recycled redwood soffits and exposed cast-in-place concrete walls, helps to make this design perfectly at home in its rustic hillside setting.

Photography: Russell Abraham

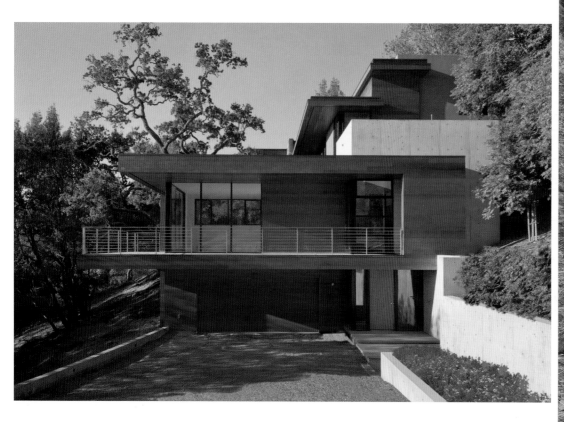

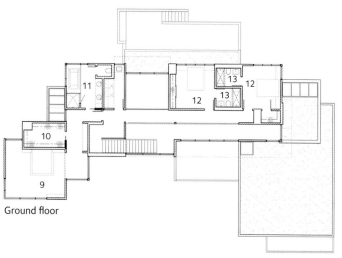

Ground floor

First floor

1 Entry
2 Study
3 Water closet
4 Lounge
5 Dining room
6 Kitchen
7 Family room
8 Terrace
9 Master bedroom
10 Walk-in wardrobe
11 Master ensuite
12 Bedroom
13 Ensuite

0   4m

Mount Coot-tha House

Shaun Lockyer Architects
Mount Coot-tha, Brisbane, Australia

The house sits on a site surrounded by national park and mountain yet only 7 kilometres (4.5 miles) from the centre of Brisbane. The site, some 1300 square metres (14,000 square feet) in area, permitted only a 400-square-metre (4300 square feet) building envelope within which to build, owing to existing planning covenants. The brief called for a large family home for six people that needed to work within these constraints, as well as the dramatic topography of the site, while taking advantage of the north-facing relationship with the bush.

The driving factor behind the design was the outdoor space that is the focus of the living areas, as well as the connection point to the bush to the north. The swimming pool sits in front of the outdoor living space and forms part of the view out over the bush. The house itself is organised into a series of functional zones – children's bedrooms, master bedroom, formal living and service areas – that hang off a circulation core on one end and the large outdoor space on the other. The design plays with a series of volumetric and spatial ideas that afford a variety of light qualities, variation in the qualities of space and overall experience of the house. A liberal approach to scale creates a range of spaces from large and public to smaller and more intimate.

The primary living area occupies the eastern edge of the property and is an extruded tall volume that connects the northern and southern edges of the house. The site enjoys light and sun all day long, affording year-round comfort. The kitchen occupies pride of place in a central location, directly facing outdoor space. Large transparent bi-fold doors dissolve any sense of the indoor and outdoor relationship. The kitchen serves as the nexus point between formal and informal living on one hand, and the circulation core and outdoor areas on the other. Bedrooms occupy the upper floor and focus around an internal void lit from above that allows visual and acoustic connection to the living areas below. A sub-floor accommodates garaging and a guest/media area that connects directly to the bush, thanks to the twisting site topography.

The building materials are deliberately restrained and intended to limit ongoing maintenance for the busy owners. Dark lightweight cladding connects the house to the bush visually, while the bulk of the white rendered walls address the more urban face of the house. Selected application of Australian hardwoods brings a softer and more crafted element into the house and forms part of the philosophical transition between bush and house. The roof-forms are bold and reflect the topography of the site; the pitch of the roof maximises collection of rainwater and absorption of solar rays.

Photography: Aperture Photography

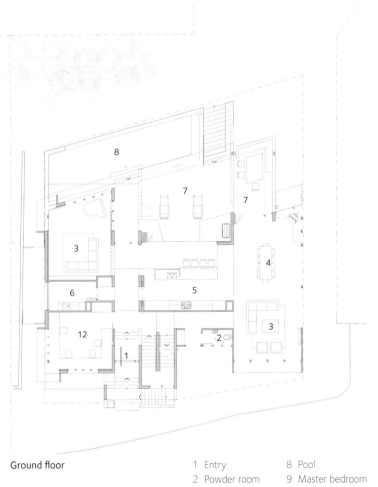

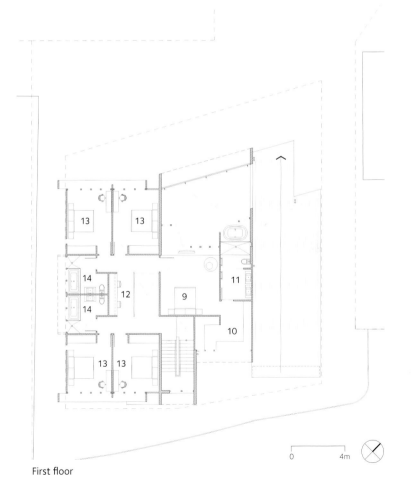

Ground floor

First floor

1 Entry
2 Powder room
3 Living area
4 Dining area
5 Kitchen
6 Laundry
7 Deck

8 Pool
9 Master bedroom
10 Walk-in wardrobe
11 Ensuite
12 Study
13 Bedroom
14 Bathroom

Mountain Range House

Irving Smith Jack Architects
Brightwater, Nelson, New Zealand

Situated at the foot of the Richmond Ranges, on New Zealand's South Island, Mountain Range House forms an enclosed verandah providing new living space for an inter-generational family between their existing farmhouse and pool. Whereas the farmhouse holds tight contained spaces within perimeter walls, the new open and elongated transition spaces connect and inform living with the landscape. Like the mountain ranges above them, the new house concertinas in silhouette to define connected sitting, dining and kitchen areas within a single communal space for all the family to converge and spread out as they wish.

Mountain Range House explores the relationship between horizontal planes parallel and transitioning to the landscape, and the holding and releasing of the space between shape and timber materiality, to allow a collection of primary living spaces to function as a single verandah area.

This single transition space is articulated in a series of living areas through volume and light rather than between walls. Each ceiling fold defines programme space, connecting in series parallel to the landscape. Volume continuously responds to the exterior environment, with light captured through full-length northeastern glazing, differentiated by perimeter wall dividers and external sun-screening, and then held and released between warming horizontal timber ceiling and flooring planes. Hoop pine, poplar and maple finishes combine richness and an inviting aspect to counter the open scale and rear concrete walls, which orientate the interior outwards to the landscape while providing thermal mass to stabilise the large open-plan environment.

Mountain Range House's internal living verandah provides maximum connection to the exterior landscape while providing an inviting and articulated series of living spaces, each gaining immediate and ever-changing architectural quality from the exterior.

Photography: Patrick Reynolds

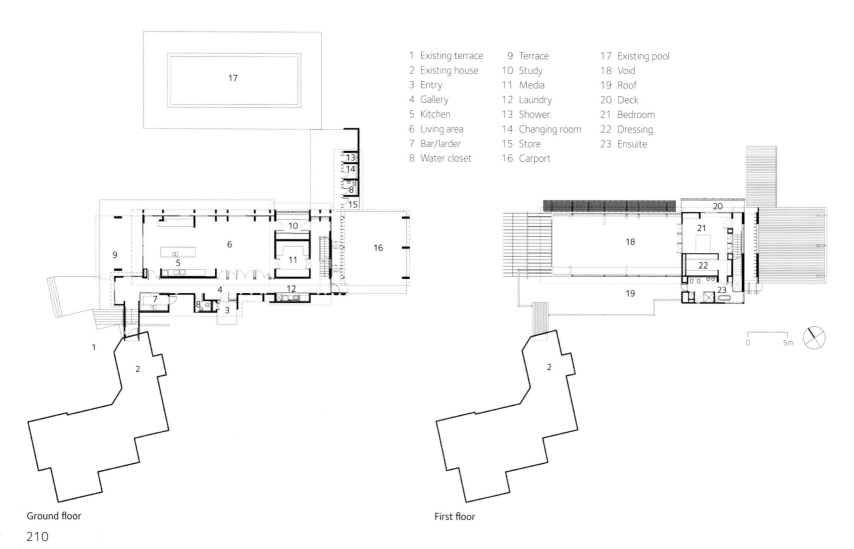

1 Existing terrace	9 Terrace	17 Existing pool
2 Existing house	10 Study	18 Void
3 Entry	11 Media	19 Roof
4 Gallery	12 Laundry	20 Deck
5 Kitchen	13 Shower	21 Bedroom
6 Living area	14 Changing room	22 Dressing
7 Bar/larder	15 Store	23 Ensuite
8 Water closet	16 Carport	

Ground floor

First floor

N85 Residence

The house as platform has been used to investigate two issues central to design today: the family as a social unit; and the environment. The lifestyle of the Indian family has changed in the age of global travel and the internet, with new spatial needs and notions of comfort. Local resources are often at odds with shifts in lifestyle. The designers demonstrate that it is possible to meet challenges of lifestyle and the environment with creative panache.

The house sets about to create its own terrain – a veritable oasis – within its inscribed territory. The forecourt is landscaped with gracious steps and pools. Crisp clear planes are articulated with materials: stone, wood and concrete, which are simply striated or set in interlocking patterns. They come alive when light hits the different horizontal surfaces. Transparency is achieved not only by glass, but a combination of water, reflection, and modulated lighting. At night the house appears magical, glowing like a lantern and allowing glimpses of activity within.

This residence multi-tasks as a house for three generations of a family and their many visitors; a busy workspace; and on occasion a cultural hub. The house is split into three levels: the private domain of the nuclear family (bedrooms and breakfast room), the shared inter-generational spaces such as the family room, kitchen and dining areas, and the fluid public domain of the lobby and living spaces. The public domain is activated each time the house opens its doors for 'Manthan,' a cultural event that promotes an energetic exchange of ideas between various creative disciplines.

One navigates the complex programme of the house through a series of spatial episodes that are expressed via volumes. These episodes are distributed across the house, revealed at chosen moments: when descending, steps cascade to subterranean offices or rooms and furniture framed by large picture windows. Moving through the house, it is clear that the central space is the fulcrum of the project. The ceiling is dotted by circular skylights with an interior garden below – a green sanctuary within the house. A lap pool fed by harvested rainwater runs the length of the terrace on the second floor.

The house is imagined as a porous object where air movement and visual connectivity permeate into the built form. The planning, orientation, structure and materiality of the house respond to the essential energy-efficient techniques suitable to the Delhi climate. It incorporates high thermal mass in the west, earth damping for the basement studios, landscape buffers on the south, high-performance surfaces on the east and the lap pool that helps with heat absorption on the top terraces. There is an entire eco-system living and growing in the heart of the house.

Photography: André J. Fanthome, Amit Mehra, Edmund Sumner

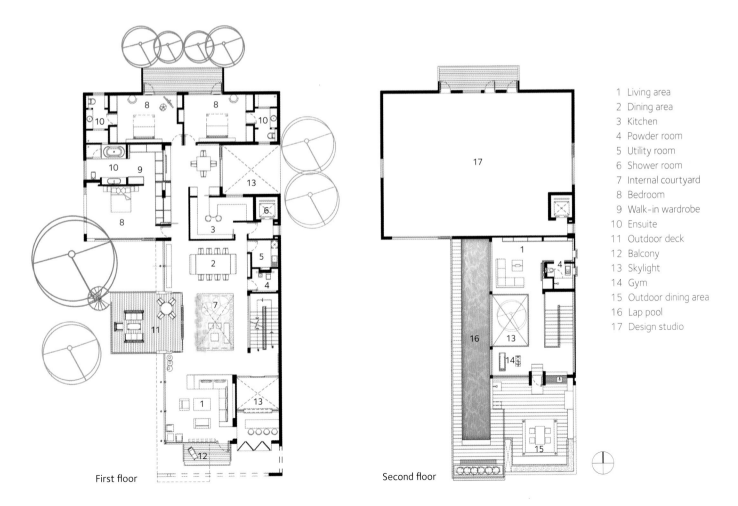

First floor

Second floor

1 Living area
2 Dining area
3 Kitchen
4 Powder room
5 Utility room
6 Shower room
7 Internal courtyard
8 Bedroom
9 Walk-in wardrobe
10 Ensuite
11 Outdoor deck
12 Balcony
13 Skylight
14 Gym
15 Outdoor dining area
16 Lap pool
17 Design studio

Nashville House

Kanner Architects
Nashville, Tennessee, USA

Responding to the client's desire for a home that would stand out from its site as a sculpture in the landscape, Nashville House provides an opportunity to design a modern home in a city with a history of traditional architecture. In certain lights it appears to rise straight out of the hillside.

The vivid white form eases itself into the natural site with the help of wood-panel cladding. Situated on a steeply sloping site, the house's vertical structure belies its lean, horizontal appearance through strategic programming. The top two living levels are cantilevered over the lower two levels, containing the home theatre and garage. The placement of a porte-cochère directs visitors up the slope and drops them among the two main levels of the house.

The master bedroom, contained in the upper-most level along with the library/study and a second bedroom, overlooks the living room below. Through an expansive wall of glass and trees beyond, one has a panoramic view of downtown Nashville.

Photography: Nicholas O. S. Marques

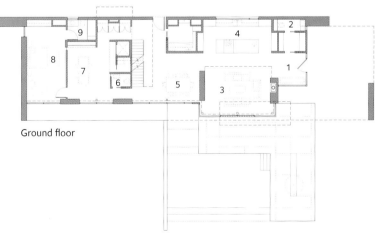

Ground floor

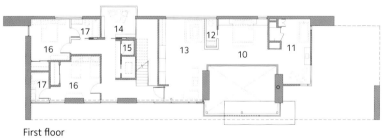

First floor

1 Entry
2 Powder room
3 Living area
4 Kitchen
5 Dining area
6 Water closet
7 Guest living area
8 Guest bedroom
9 Guest ensuite

10 Master bedroom
11 Master ensuite
12 Master water closet
13 Dressing room
14 Gallery
15 Shower room
16 Bedroom
17 Ensuite

0   3m

Nove 2

Studio B Architects
Aspen, Colorado, USA

This house is a direct response in form to its small trapezoidal lot that sat vacant for years, given the many restraints and complexities of the site. It is bound on two sides by streets with snow-storage easements and was bisected by Aspen's main water and electric lines directly under the building footprint; this required relocation and a year of approvals and strict zoning ordinances, given its location in Aspen's historic West End.

The resulting house is a direct response to these parameters – a stone-clad 'wedge' that hints at the owners' art collection, housed primarily within its double-height space. The vaulted space not only houses art but is central to the plan and is the public locus of the house. The interplay of natural light within the 6-metre-high (20 feet) volume changes personality as the day unfolds. The site is adjacent to the Aspen Institute originally designed by Herbert Bayer and the house respects Aspen's modernist history.

The programme of 300 square metres (3200 square feet) is divided between an upper private level, the public main floor and the lower guest level with the windows and doors carefully placed to ensure privacy, capture views and avoid direct sun to protect the art. Exterior materials consist of a lightweight limestone panel system with customised aluminium windows and doors; the sober interiors reflect the client's taste. The main level extends into its limited site via the landscape and enjoys several exterior terraces and gardens.

Photography: Courtesy of Studio B Architects

Lower ground floor

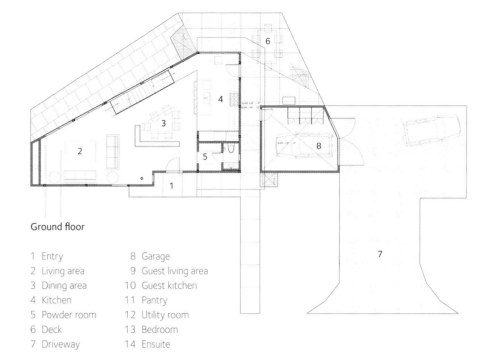

Ground floor

1 Entry
2 Living area
3 Dining area
4 Kitchen
5 Powder room
6 Deck
7 Driveway

8 Garage
9 Guest living area
10 Guest kitchen
11 Pantry
12 Utility room
13 Bedroom
14 Ensuite

Olive Tree Lane Residence

Mark English Architects
Los Altos Hills, California, USA

The Olive Tree Residence is a new home built high in the Coastal Range above the Santa Clara Valley. The site has a sweeping 270-degree view across the valley to the east. Designed for a sophisticated couple who enjoy entertaining at home, the house features an open plan with great flow.

The brightly coloured kitchen enlivens the public wing of the house, balanced by interconnected piano room, sitting room and great room. The fireplace, as might be found in a fine contemporary hotel, holds its place with the grand view outside. Subtle ceiling articulation and associated ambient lighting provide for a sense of serene theatre. Detailing and palette are simple, united by a bamboo floor.

The master bedroom and living room are lined with ivory carpeting for a more intimate feel. The contemporary bathroom features modern fixtures and dark grey tile flooring. A great element of the master bedroom is the canopy that hovers over the bed. An array of lighting shoots out from behind the canopy fixed to the wall and ceiling, and adds an ambiance of warmth to the master bedroom amid the white and grey decor.

Photography: Norma Lopez Molina

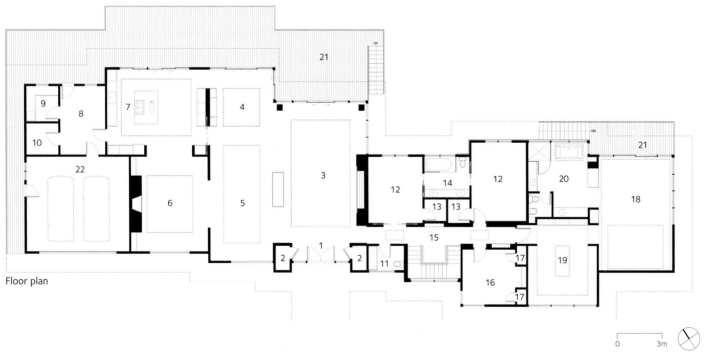

Floor plan

1 Entry
2 Coat closet
3 Living area
4 Dining area
5 Piano area
6 Family room
7 Kitchen
8 Project room
9 Laundry
10 Store
11 Powder room
12 Bedroom
13 Walk-in wardrobe
14 Ensuite
15 Hall
16 Library
17 Closet
18 Master bedroom
19 Dressing room
20 Master ensuite
21 Deck
22 Garage

0   3m

OS House

Johnsen Schmaling Architects
Racine, Wisconsin, USA

Located in an old downtown neighbourhood in Racine, Wisconsin, this house for a young family demonstrates how a small, sustainable residence can become a confident, new urban constituent, a harbinger of change in this rustbelt city suffering from decades of economic stagnation. The house occupies a narrow infill lot along the edge of Lake Michigan, completing a row of residences built over the last century.

Based on massing studies testing the building's performance in relation to site constraints, programme, accessibility to sunlight, shading, stormwater management and vegetation, the building is a simple rectangular volume that mediates between a three-storey mansion to the north and a mid-century ranch to the south.

Unlike the opaque masses of the adjacent homes, the main level glazing allows for a visual connection between street and lake. Portions of the compact mass were removed to create a number of outdoor rooms – an open entry court, elevated patios accessible from the upper level, and a shaded main-level terrace, all confined within the boundaries of the rectangular volume itself.

Along the edges of the outdoor rooms, the façade system transforms into a delicate scrim of thin aluminum rods, subtly defining the spatial boundaries of these spaces without obstructing views. A series of floor-to-ceiling apertures penetrate the façade system, their bright colours an unapologetic nod to the cheerful polychrome of the neighbourhood's Victorian homes.

The main entry facing the street is marked by a small courtyard, bracketed by a glazed vestibule on one side and the dining area on the other. The vestibule connects to a kitchen overlooking the open living area, generously glazed to frame expansive views of the lake and neighbourhood. A series of sliding glass doors provide access to a large terrace, allowing the living area to expand to the outside in summer. A central staircase leads to the upper level, where three bedrooms have access to two rooftop patios. The stairs terminate in a study cantilevering over the edge of the house, offering stunning lake views.

Photography: John J. Macaulay

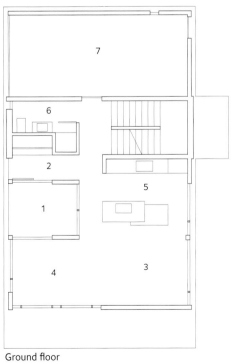

Ground floor

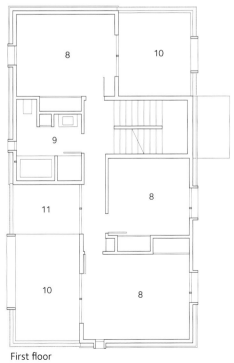

First floor

1 Front courtyard
2 Entry
3 Living area
4 Dining area
5 Kitchen
6 Powder room
7 Garage
8 Bedroom
9 Bathroom
10 Patio
11 Open to below

0   2m

OUTrial House

KWK PROMES – Robert Koniezny
Książenice, near Warsaw, Poland

A green clearing surrounded by forest was the context for the house, built for the guitarist in a rock band. Hence the idea to carve out a piece of the grass-covered site, move it up and treat it as the roof, under which to contain all required elements. As a recording artist, the client had another request – to create some space for a small recording studio and a conservatory. The latter was obtained by linking the ground floor with the grassy roof through an incision in the green plane and bending the incised fragment down inside the building.

This procedure turned the roof into an atrium, as the only way to reach it was through the interior of the house. As opposed to a typical atrium, the newly created space has all the advantages of an outer garden while remaining a safe, internal zone within the building. This way, a new type of house was created, and its designation – OUTrial –

conveys the idea of an atypical atrium that is part of both the interior and the exterior of the building.

The studio was created in a similar way as the conservatory, but in order to ensure a comfortable working environment for a rock musician, it was isolated from the rest of the house by shifting it upwards.

The smoothly curving roof creates a space similar to a bandstand that can be used for outdoor jam sessions. A very similar process was used to design the recording studio – the green roof was cut a notch and bent up, which created perfect space for a rock musician to work in. The green roof reduces the loss of heat in winter and cools the house in summer, assuring a positive microclimate inside the house.

Photography: Juliusz Sokołowski

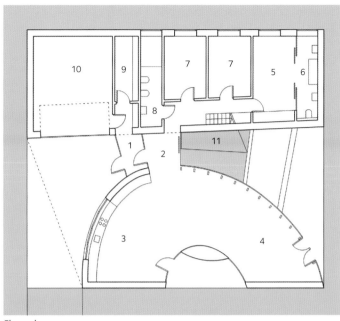

1 Entry
2 Hall
3 Kitchen/dining area
4 Living area
5 Master bedroom
6 Ensuite
7 Bedroom
8 Bathroom
9 Store
10 Garage
11 Staircase to green roof

Floor plan

0   3m

Padaro Beach House

B3 Architects, a Berkus Design Studio
Santa Barbara, California, USA

The architect's goal was to create a sustainable and multi-generational structure, bringing family together in separate enclaves within the residence. One challenge presented during the design process was to buffer noise created by the nearby freeway and railroad track adjacent to the main entry of the site. This led to the creation of an interior courtyard to serve as a modern retreat from wind and exterior sound.

The courtyard, inspired by the early California haciendas, creates a private oasis screened from neighbours, trains and traffic, and becomes the core of the dwelling. The sustainable design employs a simple palette of durable materials, precisely detailed. By utilising recycled surfaces and reclaimed materials, the structure becomes a responsible dwelling with an energy-efficiency performance exceeding California state requirements by some 50 per cent.

Careful attention was paid to the development of personal enclaves for extended family and guests alike. Separate stairways and gathering areas were created to allow retreats within the dwelling, while separate wings provide the varied residents with the independence to come and go as they please, and enjoy a variety of activities without disturbing each other.

The home is sited with southern exposure in order to take advantage of solar gain in a cool ocean environment. Operable north-facing glass is utilised to facilitate thermal siphoning, creating air movement and exhausting any undue drop in temperature within the structure. Precise and contemporary yet appropriate for an informal beach lifestyle, this home speaks to regional traditions while clearly being of its own time.

Photography: Ciro Coelho

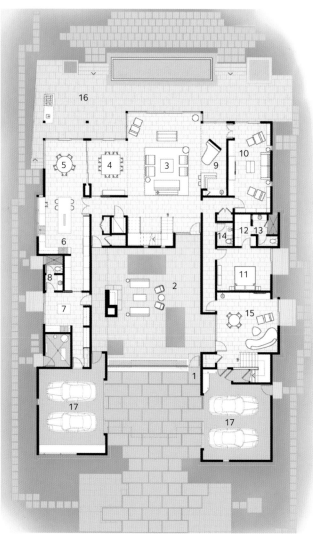

Ground floor

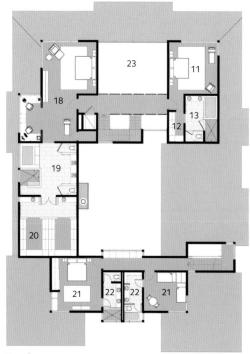

First floor

1 Entry
2 Courtyard
3 Great room
4 Dining area
5 Breakfast area
6 Kitchen
7 Laundry
8 Bathroom
9 Music area
10 Media room
11 Guest bedroom
12 Walk-in wardrobe
13 Guest ensuite
14 Powder room
15 Multi-generational living area
16 Deck
17 Garage
18 Master bedroom
19 Master ensuite
20 Master dressing room
21 Multi-generational bedroom
22 Ensuite
23 Void

0   4m

Pavilniai Regional Park

Architektų biuras, G. Natkevičius ir partneriai
Vilnius, Lithuania

In the Middle Ages the area in Vilnius where the house is situated was a cannon foundry. The modern-day site which the client bought contained an old yellow-brick lodge. Cleaning the plaster of the lodge revealed that it had been built with bricks manufactured in a old Vilnius brick factory. Because of the historical and physical value of the structure, the original fabric of the house was preserved by wrapping it with an outer skin made of glass.

The owner of the house in Vilnius is a banker and antique book collector, who inhabits the house with three other members of his family, and wanted to make a feature of his collection of books. The house features a library containing the owner's collection of antique books located in the basement of the historical lodge. On the ground floor, which is modelled on the yard of a historical lodge, are the children's bedrooms, while the attic houses the master bedrooms. On the ground floor are the living room, kitchen, dining room and a walk-in wardrobe. In the glass-fronted basement is a Turkish bath with water closet and a garage with space for two cars.

Glass form is not an end in itself – from each point on the ground floor are stunning 360-degree views of the Pavilniai Regional Park, within whose grounds the house lies. The building is made from pre-cast reinforced concrete in a steel frame, and is heated geothermically. The staircase, fireplace and library shelves are constructed from sheet metal.

Photography: Raimondas Urbakavičius

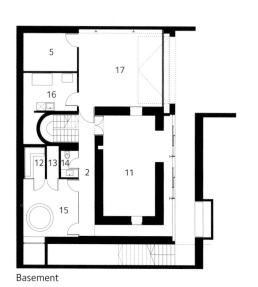

Basement

Ground floor

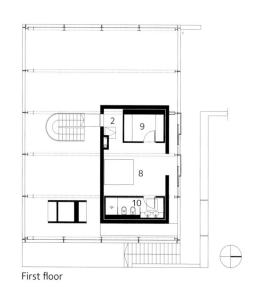

First floor

1 Entry	7 Bathroom	13 Shower
2 Hall	8 Master bedroom	14 Water closet
3 Living area	9 Walk-in wardrobe	15 Changing room
4 Dining area/kitchen	10 Ensuite	16 Turkish bath
5 Store	11 Library	17 Garage
6 Bedroom	12 Sauna	

Peninsula House

Keith Pike Associates
Sydney, New South Wales, Australia

The site is located on a peninsula that has a single access road projecting far out into Sydney's western harbour. The land falls steeply towards the water from the road, with the house located at the top of the site. The house faces due north and enjoys expansive harbour views in all directions. Sandstone-faced retaining walls support a series of stepped garden levels down to the water's edge.

The art-loving clients commissioned noted sculptor Bert Flugelman to create an inspired stainless steel piece for the waterfront lawn. The house is organised on each of its three levels around a central stair hall

that has a specially designed staircase featuring frameless, cantilevered glass treads.

At every opportunity the house opens up to the harbour view and using the shade from extensive concrete cantilevered floors and deep roof overhangs, all north-facing glass is afforded sun-protection during summer. The cross-section allows for cross-ventilation on each floor and roof water is harvested for garden irrigation and car washing. Floor levels throughout are paved in limestone, and this continues seamlessly outdoors onto extensive roof decks, balconies and garden-level terraces.

Through considered material selection, with the roof and upper level clad in standing seam copper, in combination with extensive use of sandstone facing at the lower levels and select red cedar timber features, this house responds to both site topography and the built form of neighbouring structures, with appropriate due deference.

Photography: Adrian Boddy, Keith Pike, Nuance Photography

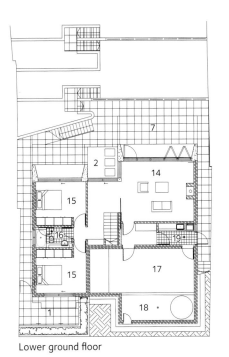

Lower ground floor

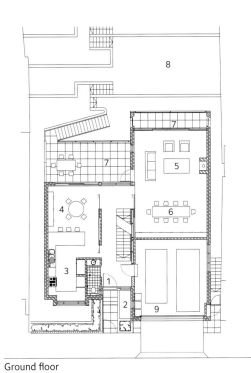

Ground floor

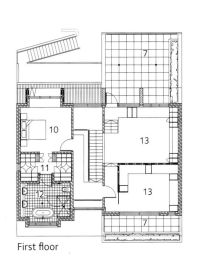

First floor

1 Entry
2 Fish pond
3 Kitchen
4 Breakfast area
5 Living area
6 Dining area
7 Terrace
8 Garden
9 Garage
10 Master bedroom
11 Walk-in wardrobe
12 Master ensuite
13 Study
14 Family room
15 Bedroom
16 Ensuite
17 Gym
18 Tank room
19 Laundry

0   5m

The Pierre

Olson Kundig Architects
Lopez Island, Washington State, USA

The owner's affection for a stone outcropping on her property inspired the design of this house. Conceived as a retreat nestled into the rock, The Pierre (the French word for stone) celebrates the materiality of the site. 'Putting the house in the rock follows a tradition of building on the least productive part of a site, leaving the best parts free for cultivation,' lead architect Kundig says. From certain angles, the house, with its rough materials, encompassing stone, green roof, and surrounding foliage, almost disappears into nature.

To set the house deep into the site, portions of the rock outcropping were excavated through a combination of machine work and handwork. The contractor used large drills to set the outline of the building, then used dynamite, hydraulic chippers, wire saws and other hand tools, working with finer and finer implements as construction progressed. Excavated rock was reused as crushed aggregate in the concrete flooring. Excavation marks were left exposed on all the stonework, a reminder of the building process, while huge pieces of rock were employed for the carport structure.

With the exception of a separate guest suite, the house functions on one main level, with an open-plan kitchen, dining and living space. A wood-clad storage box transitions from outside to inside; its two large bookcases open to provide concealed access to laundry and kitchen storage. A large pivoting steel and glass door provides access to a terrace. Set at a right angle to the main space, a master suite features a custom-designed bed with a leather headboard and footboard set in the middle of floor-to-ceiling bookshelves.

Throughout the house, the rock protrudes into the space, contrasting with the luxurious textures of the furnishings. Interior and exterior fireplace hearths are carved out of existing stone; levelled on top, they are otherwise left raw. In the master bathroom, water cascades through three polished pools – natural sinks in the existing stone. Off the main space, a powder room is carved out of the rock; a mirror set within a skytube reflects natural light into the space. The materiality of the built structure – mild steel, smooth concrete and drywall – create a neutral backdrop for the interior furnishings and artwork, and the exterior views to the bay.

Photography: Benjamin Benschneider

1 Entry
2 Breakfast area
3 Kitchen
4 Dining area
5 Living area
6 Pantry
7 Laundry
8 Foyer
9 Powder room
10 Bedroom
11 Ensuite
12 Master bedroom sitting area
13 Master bedroom
14 Master ensuite
15 Terrace
16 Kitchen terrace

Floor plan

Private Residence and Guest House in the Laurentian Mountains

Saucier + Perrotte Architectes
Laurentians, Québec, Canada

This single-family residence and guest house is located near the ski slopes of Mont-Tremblant in the Laurentian mountain range north of Montreal. Overlooking a verdant mountain landscape and located on the edge of a traditional log-house development, the house is uncompromising in its contemporary architectural expression, reflecting both modernity and local building traditions. The house's three main volumes, dedicated to the three lives of its occupants – eating, sleeping and living – slide on one another along an east–west axis.

Pierced obliquely by an interior staircase, the superimposed volumes are aligned with the entry-level pool. A translucent screened outdoor living room, typical of the region, projects into the woods at the point where the main volumes overlap, and emphasises the sliding geometry of the project. The residence is placed within a fold of the landscape, creating an intimate exterior space framed by the north façade of the house and a 3-metre high (10 feet) rock outcrop. Inserting the building into the forest resists the temptation to vie for a more conventional open setting and allows for several practical advantages in terms of exposure to the public realm, the sun and wind.

Situated along the same horizontal plane as the entrance volume of the main house, the guest house is envisaged as a prism, formally analogous to the building blocks of the house, having slid westward, detaching from the main mass. Erosion, a process that naturally occurs in mountainous regions, seems to have caused the volumes to glide laterally, each out of sync with the other, yet together forming a practical and harmonious composition.

The residence seeks out the infinite information from elements belonging to the site. Its surfaces respond to the specificity of the wooded site, where the verticality of the trees and tones of grey, brown, and green predominate. The north façade reflects this dense context through irregularly spaced, rough-cut strips of wood. While providing a unique façade pattern, the positioning of these strips permits several partially hidden slit window openings. The south façade, which screens the sun to varying degrees, is completely open to forest panorama. The lateral wood-slats on this face of the building form a continuous band of wall, soffit and roof deck. Roughness and a preference for the natural, in both the interior and exterior finishes, acknowledge the craft of local building trades and create an unexpected element of nature within an overall precise geometric form.

'Rooms' find themselves somewhere between flowing and compartmentalised, offering the occupants multi-purpose or interpretive spaces. The formal movement of building elements is activated by the literal movement of people in space: whether approaching by car, descending the oblique staircase, swinging the large sliding doors or swimming lengths across the pool.

Photography: Marc Cramer

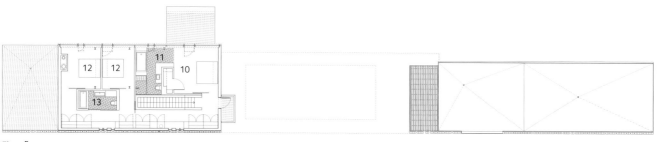

First floor

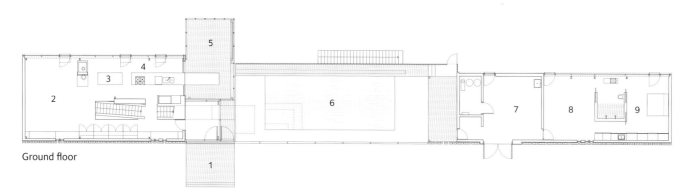

Ground floor

1 Entry
2 Living area
3 Dining area
4 Kitchen
5 Screened-in porch
6 Pool
7 Guest living area
8 Guest bedroom
9 Guest ensuite
10 Master bedroom
11 Master ensuite
12 Bedroom
13 Bathroom

0   4m

Quietways

Graham Jones Design
Victoria, Australia

Unashamedly contemporary, the simplicity of form and materials allow this house to sit placidly within its rural setting. The house is deliberately understated and disciplined, with efforts made to balance comfort with necessities and fully engage in an exploration of intimate responses to landscape, preservation of site and the optimisation of views.

Having spent time living on-site in an existing humble tin shed, the owners were familiar with the qualities (and the challenges) of the site. Their brief to the designers was for a contemporary reinterpretation of the country vernacular that actively engages with the landscape by creating unique opportunities for dramatic views, absolute privacy and tranquility.

In a carefully choreographed entry sequence, site access is gained through a sweeping driveway that gently weaves guests through existing sheds and towards the house while discretely withholding the expansive northerly view across a large dam, farmed fields and wooded hillsides.

To take advantage of the views, the living areas and master bedroom run lengthwise to compose most of the plan of an elongated cranked timber box that has been angled (both in plan and elevation), to cradle the banks of the dam and to set up dialogue with the slope of the site. A separate private zone and garage anchor each end of the main building form.

Expression of form is signified by differentiations in materiality. The timber volume is suspended, creating an elevated viewing platform, while the Corten steel and raw render volumes anchor the house to the land. The claddings are allowed to weather and are applied in a natural and subtle manner. Expansive glazing allows the landscape to fill the interiors. With a carefully considered approach, a harmonious relationship between a modest family home and a delicate site is established.

Photography: Luke Brice, Chris Groenhout

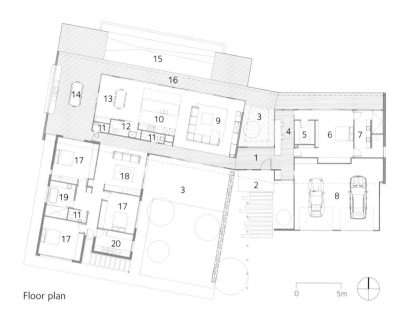

Floor plan

1 Entry
2 Porch
3 Courtyard
4 Study
5 Walk-in wardrobe
6 Master bedroom
7 Ensuite
8 Garage
9 Living room
10 Kitchen
11 Powder room
12 Pantry
13 Dining room
14 Outdoor room
15 Pool
16 Deck
17 Bedroom
18 Family room
19 Bathroom
20 Laundry

0   5m

Robinson Road Residence

Steve Domoney Architecture
Hawthorn, Victoria, Australia

Two defining notions drove the design for this new home in Hawthorn, a suburb of Melbourne. Firstly, the recognition that the street is currently in transition with the post-war brick bungalow-style dwelling, giving way to more contemporary dwellings. Secondly, with the establishment of a larger family home on the site than currently exists, the need to balance the perception of openness from within against a heightened need for privacy with the greater intensity of development now surrounding the site.

In addressing the transitional quality of the streetscape, attention is given to how a new building will fit into a likely new streetscape rather than the existing one. This rationale is evident in the resulting and somewhat 'self-confident' presence of the new home, awaiting the tide of new developments on each of its flanks.

Issues of perceived visual bulk have been addressed through the upper level by way of fragmentation along its length into three distinct sections, running front to back. Smooth white rendered cube-like forms, fore and aft, are separated midway by a lower linking section, punctuated by contrasting dark bandsawn timbers.

Issues of privacy to and from the street are addressed with the upper-level introduction of a deep terrace fronting the home office. Distant views are gained from within this space across the terrace, while the terrace acts as a visual foil, blocking sight lines from the street to this private space.

Deeper into the site and the internal spaces of the house, views are channelled from within to private outdoor living areas, while screening along its flanks prevents viewing opportunities to and from neighbouring dwellings. A balance is struck between the need for openness and requirement for privacy.

The central core of the house invites casual family living, rising through two levels; the space is defined by the proximity of the external pool, which extends to its wall face. With an overhead bridge link traversing this internal space, strong visual interconnection is achieved throughout the living zones.

Photography: Derek Swalwall Photography

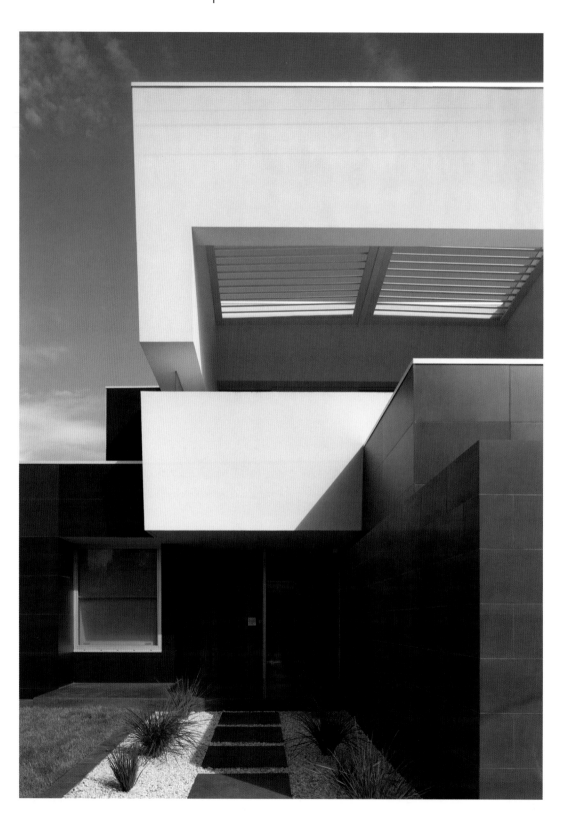

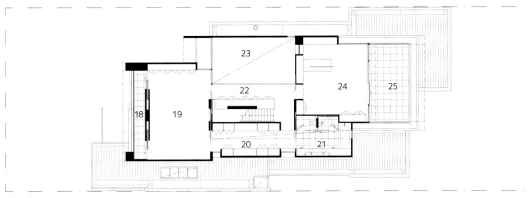

First floor

Ground floor

1 Entry
2 Store
3 Cellar
4 Theatre
5 Lounge
6 Dining Area
7 Kitchen
8 Preparation area
9 Laundry
10 Powder room
11 Bedroom
12 Bathroom
13 Drying court
14 Sundeck
15 Pool
16 Garage
17 Garden
18 Terrace
19 Master bedroom
20 Dressing room
21 Master ensuite
22 Catwalk
23 Void
24 Study
25 Balcony

0   3m

Rosalie House | **Richard Kirk Architect**
Brisbane, Queensland, Australia

This house is located in one of Brisbane's most established inner-city suburbs. The five-bedroom family home sits within a hillside among the peaks and gullies that characterise the suburb of Paddington. Rosalie House has a solid base that rises up as a three-storey lightweight structure. The exterior is predominantly recycled tallow-wood weatherboard and pre-weathered zinc cladding – the architect's contemporary interpretation of the timber and tin architecture that is prevalent in the area.

Sun-shading and privacy is achieved with operable timber screens and external venetian blinds that sit in front of a bespoke timber window joinery. The planning of the house is organised to address the views towards the city on the north-east side and Mount Coot-tha on the south-west. The resulting building footprint provides private courtyards and landscaped terraces adjacent to the main living spaces within.

The interior is an ensemble of red mahogany timber flooring and Jarrah timber panelling on a backdrop of white plaster walls and white-set ceilings. Environmental features of the house include solar-powered hot water; some 40,000 litres (10,550 gallons) of in-ground rainwater storage capacity for landscape irrigation; and low-energy lighting.

Photography: Scott Burrows, Aperture Architectural Photography

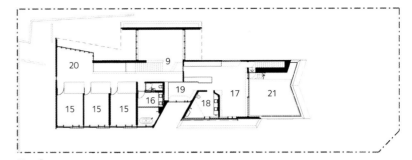

First floor

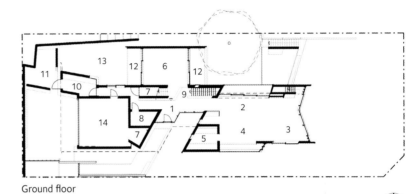

Ground floor

1 Entry	8 Powder room	15 Bedroom
2 Dining area	9 Stair	16 Bathroom
3 Living area	10 Laundry	17 Master bedroom
4 Kitchen	11 Drying court	18 Ensuite
5 Scullery	12 Terrace	19 Study
6 Gallery	13 Lawn terrace	20 Playroom
7 Store	14 Garage	21 Roof garden

Sanjaya Residence

Thomas Elliott – Paramita Abirama Istasadhya
Jakarta, Indonesia

Good synergy between the client and the architect – Tom Elliott and his team at Paramita Abirama Istasadhya – has created a large, modern, tropical-style house featuring a gallery to accommodate works of art collected by the client. Even the entry gate, main door and master bedroom door are specially designed by the noted sculptor, Rita Widagdo.

The residence is located in an exclusive neighbourhood in the south of Jakarta, sitting on more than 2000 square metres (21,500 square feet) of land. The property backs on to quiet streets on three sides, and it feels almost like being on an island when you step inside the grounds of the property.

Feng shui is the main constraint that drives the zoning of each room, and with careful design the flow from one space to another brings a different experience and ambiance, which changes depending on the time of day and the amount of natural light. Every room on the ground floor is designed with large frameless sliding doors to allows lots of natural light to enter, and for cross-ventilation to occur without the need for air-conditioning. At the same time the architect achieved a garden feel in the rooms by clever use of rock gardens and shrubbery.

To cater to the needs of privacy or entertaining, the house is divided into formal and family areas. Each bedroom has an ensuite bathroom and walk-in wardrobe. The corridor to the upper floor connects between children's areas and the master bedroom, designed like a bridge with a view to the inner courtyard. The high ceiling of the master bedroom lends a sense of spaciousness to accommodate a high four-poster bed and mosquito net.

All materials are imported stones, which when combined with solid wood used on the floor in the private areas and wooden panels in the walls, go to create a warm, intense, yet cosy house.

Photography: Ibham Jasin and Thomas Elliott

1 Main gate
2 Porte cochère
3 Foyer
4 Corridor gallery
5 Grand piano
6 Dining room
7 Living room
8 Terrace
9 Garden
10 Outdoor gallery
11 Family room
12 Breakfast room
13 Pantry
14 Koi pond
15 Guest bedroom
16 Guest walk-in wardrobe
17 Guest bathroom
18 Swimming pool
19 Study/library
20 Corridor
21 Rock garden
22 Hall
23 Void
24 Master bedroom
25 Master bathroom
26 Her walk-in wardrobe
27 His walk-in wardrobe
28 Balcony
29 Child's bedroom
30 Child's bathroom

First floor

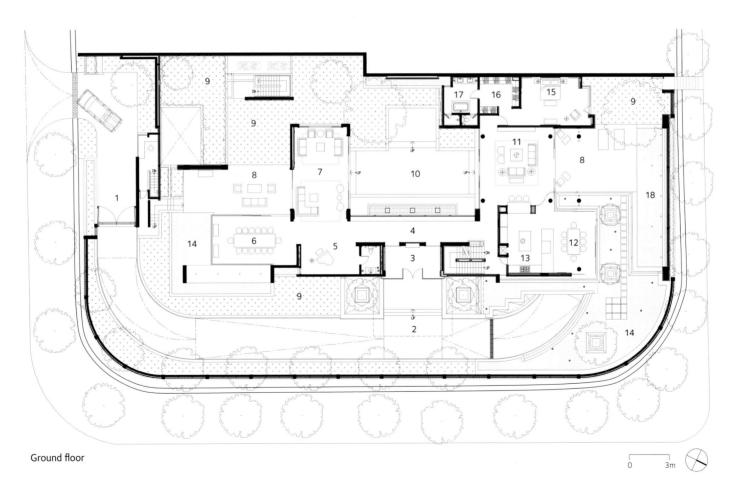

Ground floor

0   3m

Sarbonne Residence

McClean Design
Los Angeles, California, United States

Inspired by Southern California's temperate climate and the site's spectacular city views, the architect created this residence to be an entertainer's urban haven. The Sarbonne Residence's 1400-square-metre (15,000 square feet) linear one-directional layout features very high ceilings with abundant natural light and oversized windows and doors that open to the outdoors, blurring the boundary between living spaces and gardens. Multiple indoor and outdoor water features – along with a material palette consisting primarily of grey and cream stone, metals and glass – act as a tranquil unifier for the expansive home.

Rising to the home's entry from the sunken drive is a curved staircase, flanked on the left by a dark charcoal-coloured wall whose basin forms a shallow fountain spanning the length of the stairs. A grand light-filled entry, with soaring ceilings, opens to the living room. A principally white-on-white colour scheme throughout provides an ethereal canvas for select pops of colour and natural wood additions. A fireplace is inset into an east-facing polished white stone floating wall, which anchors the space.

A northeastern hallway serves as the primary path to provide access to first-floor rooms, while a hidden hallway spans the glazed southwestern façade to allow for easy navigation from kitchen to living room. As one progresses deeper into the home, white polished stone floors transition into wide-planked charcoal-toned wood floors. The darker floors act to ground the more intimate dining and open family room/kitchen, and add warmth to the massive space.

From the stair hall's ultra-modern crisp white spiral staircase treaded in charcoal-toned wood, one ascends to the upper level. The master suite comprises the western wing, while guest bedrooms, living and entertainment areas are located in the eastern wing. The designer artfully arranged all bedrooms to take full advantage of vistas and abundant natural light. To enhance the connection with the outdoors, most spaces feature floor-to-ceiling window and walls, which open to the wrap-around balconies. An expansive upper deck is placed between a secondary bedroom and guest suite to provide additional private outdoor space.

Having adequate tailored outdoor spaces was paramount to the designer, although the tight hillside lot proved to be an obstacle. McClean tackled this challenge by enlisting the use of an expansive tiered patio garden, which is supported by a series of piers. Along the southern façade, white stone from the interior is carried outside to form an expansive deck. Beyond the deck, an infinity pool frames a seemingly floating fire-feature and the water visually disappears into the hillside below. The result is a modern urban haven that 'floats' above the city below.

Photography: Jim Bartsch

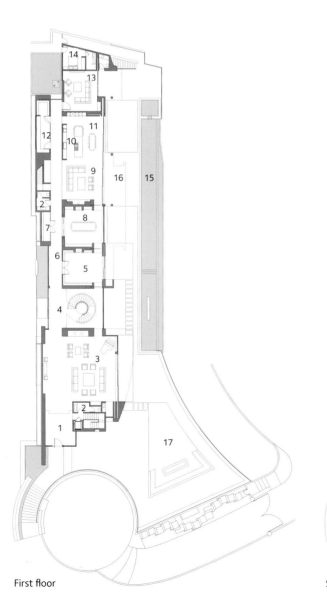

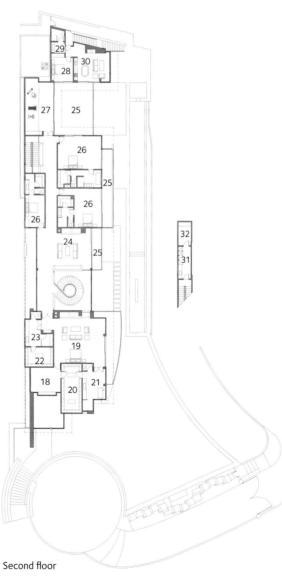

First floor

Second floor

1 Entry
2 Powder room
3 Living room
4 Stair hall
5 Library/office
6 Hall
7 Wine room
8 Dining room
9 Family room
10 Kitchen
11 Nook
12 Butler's pantry
13 Media room
14 Maid's room
15 Pool
16 Pool deck
17 Firepit
18 Office
19 Master suite
20 Master walk-in wardrobe (hers)
21 Master bathroom (hers)
22 Master walk-in wardrobe (his)
23 Master bathroom (his)
24 Living room
25 Deck
26 Bedroom
27 Gym
28 Guest bedroom
29 Guest bathroom
30 Guest suite
31 Laundry
32 Storage

0   3m

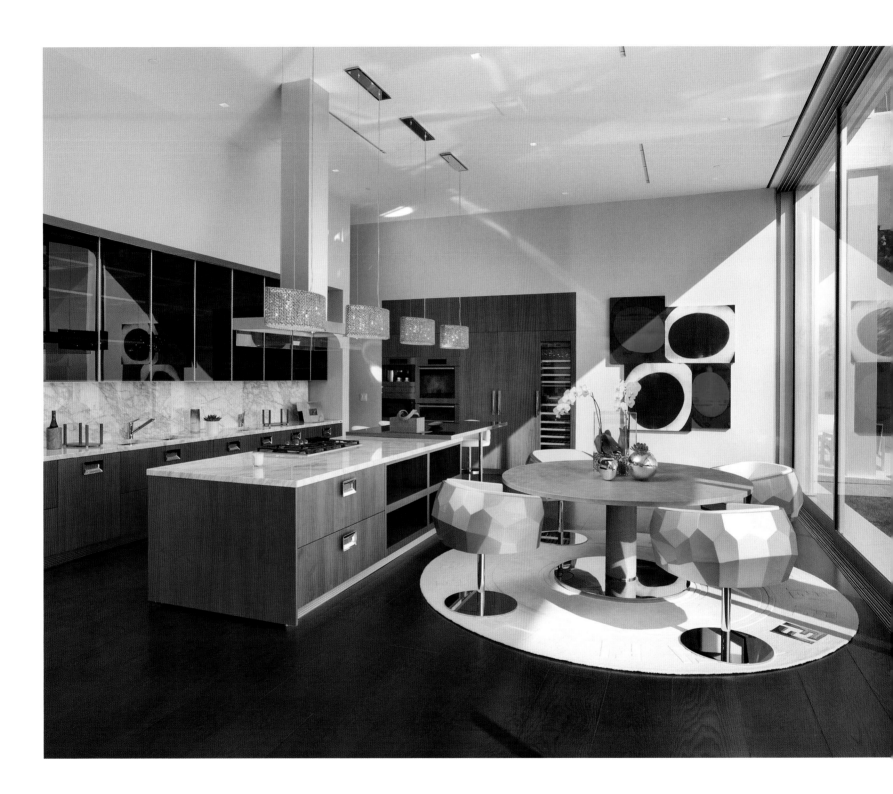

Schwartz Residence

Jon Anderson Architecture
El Paso, Texas, USA

The client wanted to build a contemporary house on an infill lot in the established Country Club neighbourhood of northwest El Paso, Texas. Together, the architect and client developed the goals of the project: to maximise the site, provide a sense of openness while maintaining privacy, and incorporate the latest in home-automation technology.

Through the orchestration of perimeter spaces, landscape elements and the site, outdoor living areas were created that feel private and protected but also open, despite the house filling the majority of the lot. Though very different from neighbouring houses, this cast-in-place concrete house responds to its environment by embracing the desert light and climate, but also by addressing the notions of scale and contrast of solid versus void inherent within the neighbourhood.

The entire vertical structure of the house is made from cast-in-place concrete. The lot is on the south side of the street with the front courtyard, parking area and entry facing north; the pool and outdoor living spaces face south. The visitor enters a large, circular courtyard, where a stainless steel gate allows access to a small entry courtyard lined with water and a water wall. A pair of stainless-steel doors open onto a 7-metre-high (22 feet) entry gallery with views out to the backyard spa and pool area. A formal dining area is on the left, with the kitchen and den area beyond. Another water wall separates the den from the rest of the house. The master suite is at the end of the entry gallery and the living room is down two steps to the right.

The exposed concrete is complemented by large glass areas and stainless steel details, while the interior offers the owner a rich environment with dark stained concrete floors, warm wood and plaster finishes and the sound of flowing water echoing through the spaces. The house is equipped with all the conveniences and comfort available through modern home-automation technology: all switches are low-voltage and programmable remotely; the house is wired for security, audio, video, and internet technology; and a handheld colour touch screen is available for the resident to see who is at the front door, to open and close window shades, to change thermostat settings and play music.

Photography: Kirk Gittings

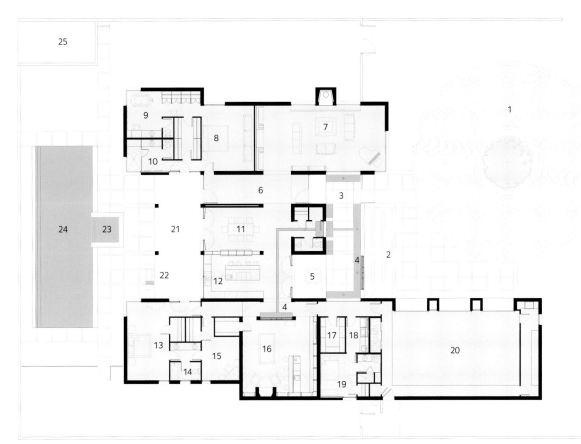

Floor plan

1 Front courtyard/parking
2 Terraced planters
3 Entry
4 Water wall
5 Patio
6 Gallery
7 Living room
8 Master bedroom
9 Her ensuite
10 His ensuite
11 Dining room
12 Kitchen
13 Guest bedroom
14 Guest ensuite
15 Office
16 Den
17 Pantry
18 Laundry
19 Maid's quarters
20 Garage
21 Outdoor dining area
22 Barbecue
23 Spa
24 Pool
25 Mechanical room

Seacliff House

Chris Elliott Architects
Sydney, New South Wales, Australia

Overlooking the ocean from the clifftop at Bronte, this house comprises four levels, each with a different purpose and character. The ground floor is essentially a transparent platform, which engages with the surroundings. Visually, nature is welcomed in. The space is ordered by a series of columns and defined by solid walls only where necessary. Glass plays along, around and above the solid elements, while large sliding and pivoting glass doors open up to outside.

The basement level is conceived as a watery grotto. The sandstone is carved away to create space. Rather than remove the material or cover it up as is often done, in places it is left to invade the space. This connects the house in an intimate way to the very essence of Sydney – its sandstone base. Water occurs at various levels – a pool, a shallow reflecting pool with a bridge and an outside bath. At times strong shafts of light penetrate the spaces, as through rock fissures in a cave. At other times when light levels are low, strong colours help to create warmth and atmosphere.

The bedroom level, conceptually a protective cocoon, is a long linear box. It provides comfort and privacy, with glimpses out through a variety of openings, with the option of one or two layers of curtains. The first is opaque, the second a translucent veil. The surface of the box is enlivened by a series of curvilinear light scoops. These allow light in and offer selective views out, such as a view of the sky when lying in the bath.

At the roof level, conceived as a belvedere or lookout, a study opens onto a small deck. Here, at the end of the journey one is rewarded with a panoramic view over the ocean. A private sundeck with built-in timber seating and a fireplace provides a comfortable place to contemplate the ocean and the stars at night.

Photography: Richard Glover

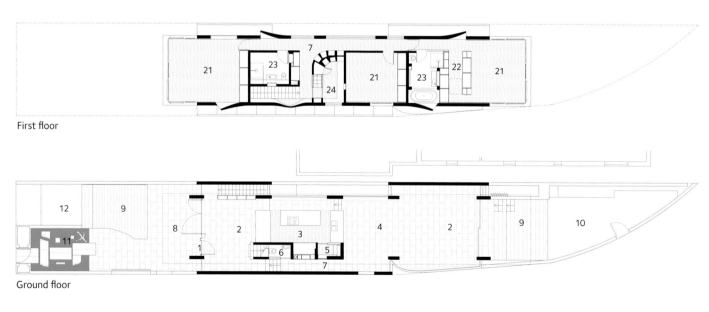

First floor

Ground floor

Basement

1 Entry
2 Living area
3 Kitchen
4 Dining area
5 Pantry
6 Water closet
7 Hall
8 Patio
9 Deck
10 Garden
11 Pond
12 Driveway
13 Garage
14 Laundry
15 Bridge
16 Shower
17 Bedroom
18 Courtyard
19 Store
20 Grotto
21 Bedroom
22 Walk-in wardrobe
23 Ensuite
24 Study

0   3m

Seneca Road Residence

Searl Lamaster Howe Architects with Joe Valerio, FAIA
Venice, Florida, USA

Located on the Gulf Coast of Florida, this ecologically sound house was recently certified at the LEED for Homes platinum level. Native scrub oak and cabbage palms that existed on the 2000-square-metre (half an acre) site were retained and invasive species were replaced with native, drought-resistant plant materials.

This holiday home was jointly designed by architect couple Linda Searl and Joe Valerio as a winter retreat. The house's highly sculptural form is clad in concrete and stucco and punctuated by commercial-grade storefront windows and doors. A standing-seam metal roof is pitched to a large concealed gutter that harvests rainwater for reuse. Other sustainable strategies include a 5-kilowatt SunPower photovoltaic array, a Heliodyne direct solar domestic hot water system, and a variety of other systems.

The main living level is 3.6 metres (12 feet) above grade and overlooks a nearby preserve and bird sanctuary. Inside the primary living space is a combined, high-ceilinged living/dining/kitchen area. South-facing windows and doors open onto a pool and are shaded by a trellis topped with solar panels to generate hot water. A screened dining porch opens onto the pool area. The concrete of the pool deck is repeated in a polished finish on the interior floors throughout.

Photography: Antonio Cuellar

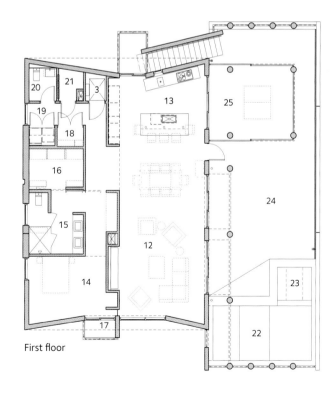

Ground floor

First floor

1 Entry portico
2 Lower deck
3 Lift
4 Bedroom
5 Ensuite
6 Pool above
7 Whirlpool above
8 Waste area
9 Mechanical room
10 Car park
11 Rainwater storage tanks
12 Great room
13 Kitchen
14 Master bedroom
15 Master ensuite
16 Walk-in wardrobe
17 Balcony
18 Closet
19 Laundry
20 Powder room
21 Store
22 Pool
23 Whirlpool
24 Deck
25 Screen porch

Sentosa House

Concrete Architectural Associates
Sentosa Cove, Singapore

The house is situated on a corner lot with two sides facing a canal. The architect's aim to celebrate this unique waterfront view was achieved by strategically locating a free-standing oval-shaped living room that anchored the project on the site, orientating it towards the water. The rest of the house is contained within a fluid and natural form and serves as a backdrop to the living space.

The swimming pool is placed within a semi-open courtyard that mediates the living room and the main form. The free-form pool is partially covered by a roof that is reminiscent of a canopy, something closely tied to the idea of tropical living that allows one to exist outside while simultaneously being protected from the elements. The large aperture in the roof, inspired by the Pantheon, allows for natural light, ventilation and precipitation into the swimming pool while giving the roof a sense of weightlessness, allowing it to 'float' above the rest of the house.

The public façade of the project was designed to seem 'faceless' for reasons of privacy as well as to provide shade from the fierce sun. The walls seem to 'peel' off the building, morphing and transforming as one passes, before becoming fenestrations facing north. The architect's brief was to emphasise the courtyard and ensure harmony between inside and out. It was important that the two melded, creating a seamless flow of circulation that occurred laterally from outdoor to indoor, as well as vertically, between floors. The entire house becomes an endless playground to meander through, always open to views of the water, yet intensely private. This seamlessness has been further realised in the project's furniture and finishings. The use of Corian allows for a continuous finish that flows through the entire house, allowing the finishing to transform into one large piece of 'furniture'.

The oval living room is the penultimate realisation of the seamless flow of movement. The swimming pool seems to slip into the living room as its mosaic tiles cover the zone where the geometries of both spaces begin to interact with each other. The lighting scheme of the room allows it to be lit in various colours throughout the day, adjusting the atmosphere of the room to suit the mood of the user. The space can either blend into the environment or become a single glowing object in the dark.

The garage, usually considered separate from a house, is instead made a cohesive part of the interior. It is unenclosed, separated from the foyer only by a glass wall. It is designed as a private display case, a mini automotive museum of sorts, where a wall of 1:24 scale cars serve as an impressive backdrop to a full-size Ferrari or Lamborghini.

Photography: Sash Alexander

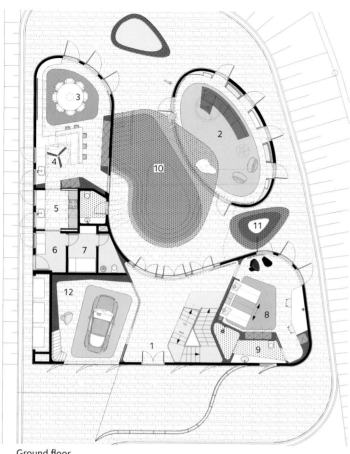

Ground floor

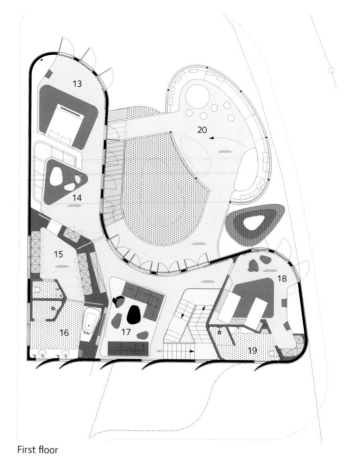

First floor

1 Entrance hall
2 Living room
3 Dining room
4 Breakfast bar
5 Kitchen
6 Pantry
7 Maid's quarters
8 Boys' bedroom
9 Boys' ensuite
10 Pool
11 Whirlpool
12 Garage
13 Master bedroom
14 Master living room
15 Dressing room
16 Master ensuite
17 Family room
18 Girls' bedroom
19 Girls' ensuite
20 Terrace

Short Residence

Diamond Schmitt Architects
Mustique, St Vincent and the Grenadines, West Indies

The residence is located on Mustique, a privately-owned island in an archipelago that forms St Vincent and the Grenadines in the West Indies. The 730-hectare (1800 acres) island has been developed as one of the world's most exclusive resorts with no more than 100 residences and a small hotel. The island is owned and operated by the Mustique Company, comprising shareholders and owners and is dedicated to protecting its natural beauty, tranquility and privacy.

The 1850-square-metre (20000 square feet) residence is organised to maximise ocean views. Situated on a steep slope, the living room, dining room and kitchen all overlook the sea. It also incorporates six bedrooms, a gym, pool, spa and activity rooms. Wide eaves for all buildings give protection from the sun and rain. As there is no groundwater on Mustique, all water is collected from the roofs. The protective roof, therefore, is of both symbolic and practical importance.

There are three main levels to the house, cascading in three giant steps down the slope of the site. Each succeeding level, projecting beyond the structure above and cantilevered beyond the supporting columns or walls below, provides generous decks and terraces, as well as affording protection from sun and rain. Access to the main living rooms of the house, located in the middle of the three levels, is gained by a path from the visitor parking area via a bridge over a depression on the site. This natural storm watercourse has been utilised to feed a fishpond, waterfall and stream.

The entrance portal frames a view of the spectacular east coast of the island. There are no doors as such, due to a climate in which breeze is at a premium. Passing through this portal reveals the full panorama of the coast, coral reef and seascape. The living room is backed by a stone retaining wall, which contrasts with an entirely open wall to the south, giving prominence to the open-air configuration that defines the residence.

The upturned beams of the flat roofs support the surface decking, which in its turn shades the concrete roof slabs below, thus providing a cool enclosure to the internal spaces. Access to the upper level is given to vehicular traffic for service access to the kitchen, garages and the owner's office, as well as the upper dining room and terrace. To ensure privacy, access through the villa is gained only by way of a central staircase that bisects all levels of the house. Entry to this staircase originates on the lowest, more private level of the residence. It is at this lowest level that games room, gymnasium, children's playroom and bedrooms and the separate master bedroom suite are situated.

Photography: Tom Arban

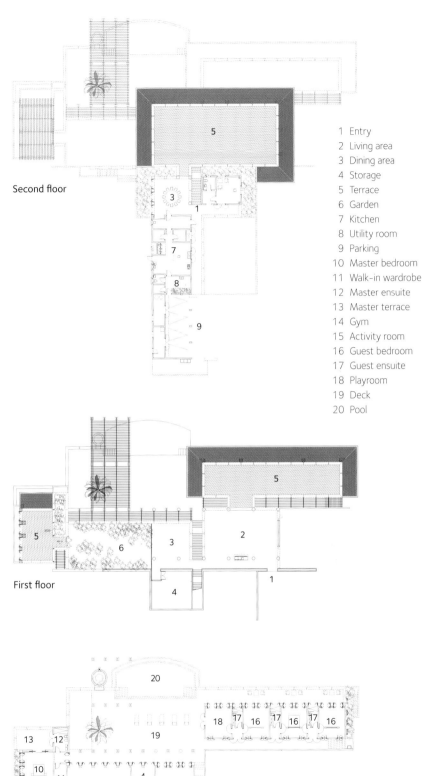

Second floor

1 Entry
2 Living area
3 Dining area
4 Storage
5 Terrace
6 Garden
7 Kitchen
8 Utility room
9 Parking
10 Master bedroom
11 Walk-in wardrobe
12 Master ensuite
13 Master terrace
14 Gym
15 Activity room
16 Guest bedroom
17 Guest ensuite
18 Playroom
19 Deck
20 Pool

First floor

Ground floor

Surf Residence

Paul Uhlmann Architects
Gold Coast, Queensland, Australia

This beachside house is nestled among a mix of beach houses and units. On a side street close to the beach, the house layout orientates towards the northern boundary to take advantage of exposure to the sun and prevailing sea breezes. A two-storey void is incorporated to allow light and ventilation to penetrate the long floor plan. This double-height void allows views toward the sky from this confined site.

Bedrooms are located on the first floor with passing views into the living area and pool below. The study is located above a curved mosaic element that houses the laundry and guest bedroom below. The study has views over the living areas below and glimpses to the beach beyond. External building elements reflect the regional character of the local beach houses of the Gold Coast.

Photography: Remco Photography

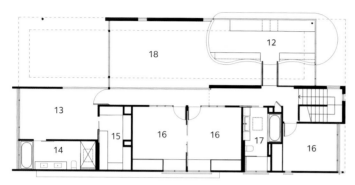

First floor

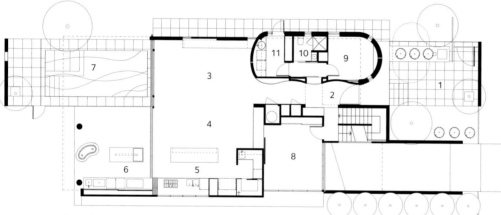

Ground floor

1 Courtyard	10 Powder room
2 Entry	11 Laundry
3 Living area	12 Study
4 Dining room	13 Master bedroom
5 Kitchen	14 Ensuite
6 Teppanyaki	15 Walk-in wardrobe
7 Pool	16 Bedroom
8 Family room	17 Bathroom
9 Guest room	18 Void

0   3m

The 22

JSª
Near Lima, Peru

The 22 house, located on a beachfront on the Pacific coast 50 kilometres (30 miles) from the Peruvian capital, Lima, comprises four beach apartments for members of the same family. The rectangular-shaped plot has a surface area of 390 square metres (4200 square feet) and truly spectacular views. To comply with the regulations of the complex, the height of the project above the seafront is about 2 metres (around 6 feet).

The common area includes swimming pool, living room, terrace and kitchen. The concept was to integrate the apartments while keeping them as independent volumes, one on top of the other, thus generating diversity in the composition of the interior and exterior spaces of each apartment. The living spaces are designed to favour the action of looking out into the open, resulting in a simplified, pared-down complex that contrasts with the privileged views.

The elongated shape of the property allowed four apartments of about 170 square metres (1830 square feet) each. The whole development is connected by a large central terrace that looks out to the most attractive view of the bay. The structural solution generates wide open spaces, without any extraneous elements, and large clearings are created with movable doors and openings that permit the interior–exterior relation to fade in and out. It is a project with a major architectural programme resolved strategically, in order to take full advantage of the rather limited space.

Photography: Eduardo Hirose

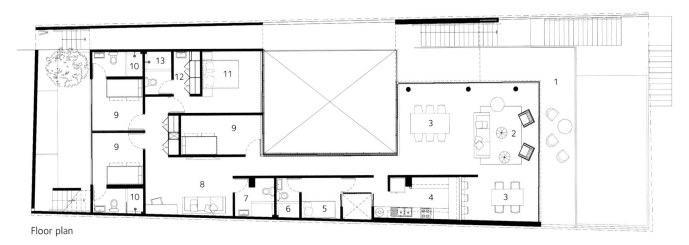

Floor plan

1 Terrace
2 Outdoor living area
3 Dining area
4 Kitchen
5 Maid's bedroom
6 Maid's ensuite
7 Water closet
8 Interior living area
9 Bedroom
10 Ensuite
11 Master bedroom
12 Walk-in wardrobe
13 Master ensuite

0   3m

Treehouse

Steendyk
Brisbane, Queensland, Australia

Treehouse derives its name from the way in which sunlight is gently dappled into the interior spaces, but also from the way environmental principles have driven the project's overall design. The replanning, refurbishment and extension of this historic 1890's worker's cottage re-engineers the house to accommodate 21st-century requirements. The client purchased the property with planning permission for an extension to the rear of the existing house, and approached the architect initially for modifications.

They required a family home for themselves and two teenage children, that could accommodate future needs such as a home office, or accommodation for a person with limited mobility. Steendyk architects suggested a more environmentally sustainable solution with a design proposal that split the building in two, creating a central courtyard that allowed for natural cross-ventilation and privacy, winter sun to penetrate the rear pavilion, passively-heated interior spaces and minimal overall energy use.

The new additions sitting either side of a grassed courtyard are steel-framed glass boxes shielded by external screens. The laser-cut Corten steel screens are active lyrical elements that dance in shape and form while filtering light and creating shade. The screens reinterpret the vernacular timber lattice screens present throughout the historic suburb of Spring Hill, Brisbane. Designed with three apertures, each plane of the screen is considered in regards to orientation, with a specific aperture – small, medium or large – assigned to suit.

Delicate stainless-steel rods project from the steel and glass boxes to hold and visually separate the exterior screens from the body of the house. Under the grassed courtyard, 25,000 litres (6600 gallons) of precious water is collected, stored, used, reclaimed and recycled, and energy from the sun is harnessed with solar cells and thermal mass for redistribution. This refurbishment preserves the historic nature of Spring Hill for future generations by respecting the original integrity of the residence.

Photography: Christopher Frederick Jones

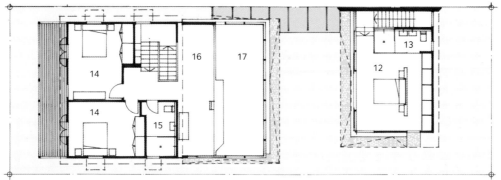

First floor

Ground floor

1 Entry
2 Office
3 Powder room
4 Store
5 Kitchen
6 Dining area
7 Laundry
8 Garage
9 Courtyard
10 Living area
11 Pool
12 Master bedroom
13 Master ensuite
14 Bedroom
15 Bathroom
16 Study
17 Void

0   3m

U House

Jorge Graça Costa Architect
Ericeira, Portugal

The U House is located in Ericeira, a major surfing resort, and designed for José Gregório, three times national surf champion of Portugal, his wife and two daughters. The 300-square-metre (3200 square feet) house occupies a large lot surrounded by a dense mesh of trees on top of a hill overlooking Saint Lorenzo Bay. The mutual interest in sustainability of architect and client did not prevent them from wholeheartedly embracing modern design. The goal was to allow aesthetics and exciting architectural solutions to predominate, instead of designing a building restricted by superfluous green technologies or merely aggregating raw materials.

The house design emerges from the inevitability of protection from prevailing winds. The north wind dominant in the summer and the stormy south wind dominant in the winter carry rain from the sea.

Therefore the central idea was a design based on the reinterpretation of traditional Mediterranean terrace houses, creating a patio sitting on a plateau embraced by two long arms interconnected by a third body, without ignoring the fabulous views to the west, even in interior spaces. Abundant glazing brings in natural light, while a high-performance envelope controls temperatures. Eco-friendly interior finishes and artwork made from recycled materials take prominent place in the house.

The numerous sustainable features include cork, which has a primary isolation material; natural heating and cooling; floor and water heating from solar panels supported by biomass heating; a microclimate environment created by the patio and the pool (pool water is not treated chemically) and rainwater harvesting (collected in a pre-existing well) for irrigation proposes.

The house's success in harmonising design, functionality and sustainability is augmented by its liveability, extreme comfort and considerable savings in consumption of water and energy. Its humble size and careful design are a testament to the successful balance of architecture with a prescriptive performance design.

Photography: FG+SG

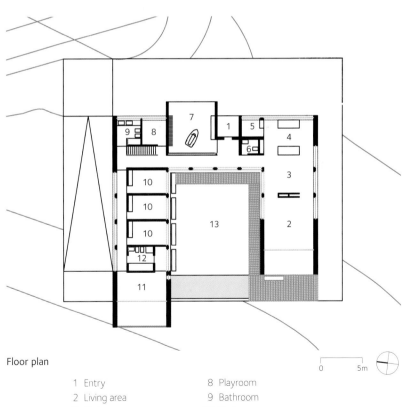

Floor plan

1 Entry
2 Living area
3 Dining area
4 Kitchen
5 Pantry
6 Water closet
7 Surfboards/trophy room

8 Playroom
9 Bathroom
10 Bedroom
11 Master bedroom
12 Master ensuite/walk-in wardrobe
13 Patio

0   5m

Victoria 73 | SAOTA – Stefan Antoni Olmesdahl Truen Architects
Bantry Bay, Cape Town, South Africa

The brief called for a dynamic response to capitalise on the site of an existing property, by creating an environment where a young family could enjoy an outdoor lifestyle protected from the prevailing winds and enjoy views of the sea and large boulders to the immediate south. The clients were eager to use every possible area of the site, yet ensure privacy in this dense part of Bantry Bay. The steep tapered shape of the plot complicated the design and hampered the construction process. The budget restrictions implied that a component of the existing building needed to be retained, which also created consequential problems in design, documentation and execution.

The design was driven primarily by the need to create a family home that accommodated the kitchen, living room and dining room in a single space. These areas enjoy all-day sunlight and frame views of the sea and adjacent rock features and connect this level to the private bedroom level above. The secondary living area is a dramatic entertainment space, located on the level immediately below the family level. The pool terrace

allows for covered and uncovered areas in which to relax. The entertainment lounge accommodates a bar, beside the outdoor braai area. A dramatic gazebo structure is perched at the western edge of the pool deck, which allows the owners to enjoy the setting sun.

The top floor accommodates the main bedroom with two children's ensuite bedrooms and a small lounge. Guest and staff accommodation as well as a private library are located on the first and second storey, below the entertainment level on the third floor. The ground floor accommodates the entry and a five-car garage. A glass lift connects the building vertically, and an external service stair connects the levels externally.

The house is strongly influenced by the Californian school of 'Case Study' houses and Miesien Planar Designs, demonstrated by the cantilever roof slab separated from the main off-shutter concrete roof soffit by a dramatic clerestory window. The slab is in turn supported by a marble-clad wall plane, reminiscent of the stone walls of the Barcelona Pavilion. The finishes

are rich and varied in other areas of the house, including timber cladding in various rooms and richly coloured mosaic finishes. The interiors are not over-designed, but effortlessly casual and sleek. Each piece of furniture was carefully considered to create a successful fusion of 20th-century design pieces with understated, customised items by Antoni Associates.

Visually, the building is enriched with the use of a number of interesting finishes and features. These include textured stone cladding on various internal and external walls. This contrasts with the roughness of the off-shutter concrete soffit to the living room, dining room and kitchen on the level below the top floor. The finishes are rich and varied in other areas of the house, including timber cladding in various rooms, and richly coloured mosaic finishes. The client's eclectic art collection plays an integral part in the interior and adds a dynamic background to the contemporary architecture.

Photography: Stefan Antoni

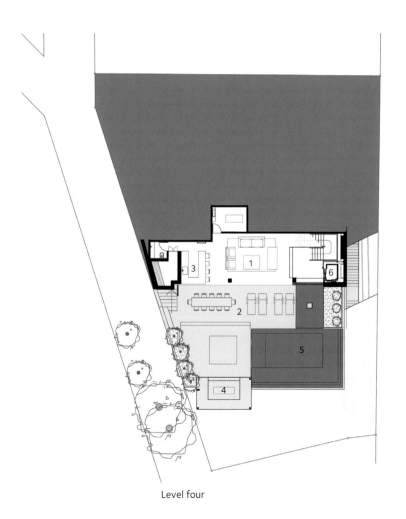

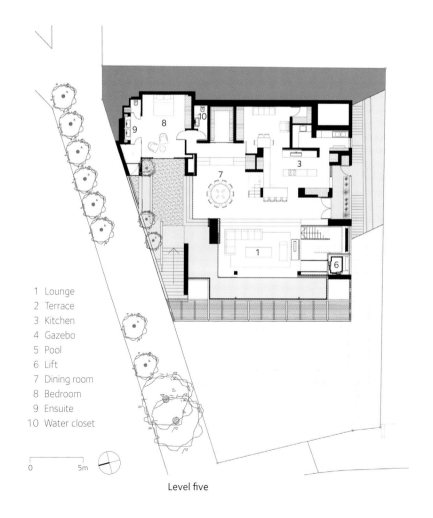

1 Lounge
2 Terrace
3 Kitchen
4 Gazebo
5 Pool
6 Lift
7 Dining room
8 Bedroom
9 Ensuite
10 Water closet

0   5m

Level four

Level five

Villa Amanzi

Original Vision
Phuket, Thailand

Nestled in a cascading, west-facing ravine with a dramatic slab of rock defining the northern edge and a stunning outlook over the azure blue of the Andaman Sea to the south, this plot presented the architect with a commission that was daunting and exciting in equal measure – to do this demanding but ultimately spectacular site justice.

The defining elements of the villa are the rock and the view, which dominate at every juncture. They resonate on first approach, through the migration from public to private space, in the living and in the family areas, and in the gardens, to the bedrooms; and they continue to command respect down the tropical jungle steps that arrive at a secluded rock platform,

flanked by the same seam that welcomes the visitor some 60 metres (200 feet) above. Constant reference to these elements instils a feeling of solidity that contrasts with the openness of the house, reinforcing the dynamism and vibrancy that pays homage to the magic of the location.

The home grows out from the rock; the bedroom element rests between it and the wing that strikes the perpendicular, rising vertically from the slope. This composition defines the open living and dining space that is simply a transition between two garden areas. It is intimate but open and the uninterrupted clear span creates a bridge, under which the conventions defining indoor space disappear.

On the lowest level, two further ensuite bedrooms are complemented by a private spa with outdoor massage bay. The large, multifunction games and theatre room gains a unique cavern-like ambiance where the rock crashes into the space, and guides one back outside and down jungle steps that lead to the ocean. Cantilevered over the massage bay, the swimming pool completes the composition. It is the focal point that draws the eye to the view and instils a calmness that provides balance with the energy of the architecture.

Photography: Marc Gerritsen and Helicam Asia Aerial Photography

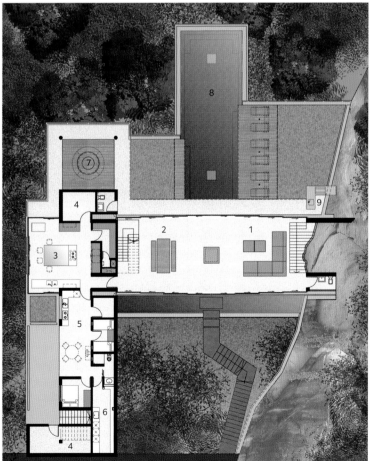

1 Living area
2 Dining area
3 Kitchen
4 Store
5 Staff quarters
6 Utility room
7 Massage area
8 Pool
9 Barbecue

0   4m

Floor plan

Villa in Kaikoh

Satoshi Okada architects
Atami, Shizuoka Prefecture, Japan

Villa in Kaikoh is designed as a vacation house for the owners to invite guests to enjoy the splendid views of the Pacific Ocean. The site is located on a cliff facing the ocean in Atami, Shizuoka Prefecture, a hot spring town 100 kilometres (60 miles) west of Tokyo. Thermal water is provided directly from its source, and inhabitants can enjoy the private spa.

The villa is composed of seven layered platforms that are continuously connected to each other like a folded ribbon, in a gesture corresponding to the convexly irregular surface of the cliff. The garage is on the top floor, which is accessed from the bridge through a gate on the street. There is an entrance inside the garage, a lift that serves all floors, and a staircase to the spa and exterior bath on the terrace. On the main entrance level there are two bedrooms and a laundry with a utility

terrace. Downstairs is a fireplace, and the living, dining and kitchen areas – the main public space in the villa. The platform is extended to the exterior terrace, from which one can appreciate the beautiful scenery of the Pacific with an almost 180-degree view.

The building has various sections that make a variety of spaces with a quality of transparency between each other. The master bedroom, bathroom and two guest rooms are one storey down from the main floor, which contains a small training room, a machinery room and a storage room. Finally, a hobby room is set in the basement, beside a small vegetable garden.

Structurally, the villa is made of steel based on a reinforced concrete structure up to the main bedroom level. There is no structural column or wall on the living

floor level, in order to eliminate any obstacle to the beautiful view of the ocean. Steel walls and slabs are composed of lattice ribs sandwiched by steel panels. Because of the difficult terrain of the steep cliff, construction had to follow a logical sequence: first, small pieces of prefabricated blocks were made in a factory, and then welded on-site. The steel blocks were suspended by a crane onto each structural element and built up, from bottom to top. Schematically, the bedroom-floor slab is suspended from the upper structure, making the solid shell of the garage.

Photography: Hiroshi Ueda

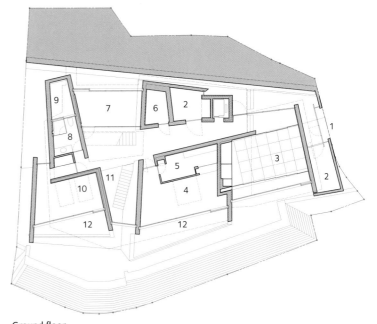

Ground floor

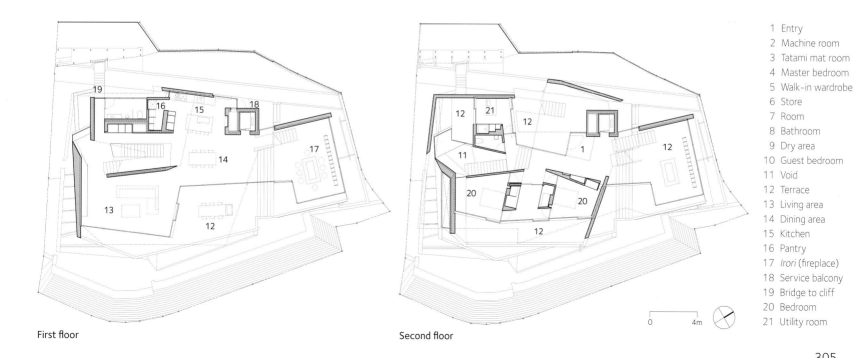

1	Entry
2	Machine room
3	Tatami mat room
4	Master bedroom
5	Walk-in wardrobe
6	Store
7	Room
8	Bathroom
9	Dry area
10	Guest bedroom
11	Void
12	Terrace
13	Living area
14	Dining area
15	Kitchen
16	Pantry
17	*Irori* (fireplace)
18	Service balcony
19	Bridge to cliff
20	Bedroom
21	Utility room

First floor

Second floor

0   4m

Villa PM

Architrend Architecture
Ragusa, Italy

The house projects its own identity through the creation of simple volumes divided among themselves. The contrast between the large windows and dark lava-stone surfaces of the ground floor and white walls of the first floor give the house the appearance of being a suspended, light volume. On the ground floor, the windows open onto the garden while on the first floor, cantilevered walls consist of sliding panels in vertical profiles of aluminium that act as a sunscreen and characterise the villa.

The angle on the roof of the villa entrance is a wall covered in lava rock and contains a cut corner – a window onto the living room. The opposite edge is made from glass and turns on the side elevation along the length of the house, with sliding glass doors to the garden that interact with the outside world in absolute transparency. On the rear of the ground floor is a more solid stone wall, alternating with a white plaster wall in the middle. The bedroom window is incised into the wall – neat, precise and sharp.

The functions are distributed in a fluid pattern. The large living room has a central atrium illuminated from above, with a palm tree in the middle – the green of outdoors extends within the house. The outdoor area of the garden is designed as a natural extension of living inside.

The outer fence is made up of a wall covered with slabs of lava; the colour is continuous along the gate and pedestrian entry on the driveway, making it completely homogeneous along the fence line.

With its sharp contemporary appearance, the villa stands out from the surrounding buildings by establishing an anomaly in space. The architect likes to think that the project is not in conflict with the environment and the landscape, but an antidote to the banality of conventional buildings.

Photography: Moreno Maggi

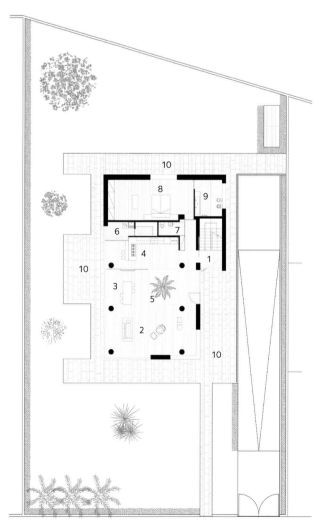

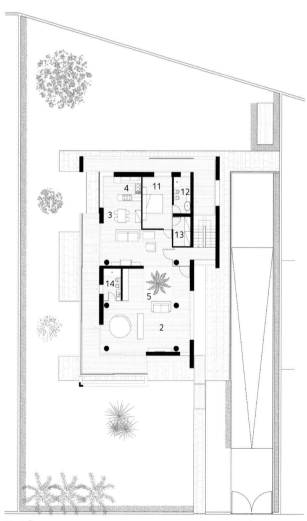

1 Entry
2 Living room
3 Dining room
4 Kitchen
5 Atrium
6 Utility room
7 Powder room
8 Master bedroom
9 Master ensuite
10 Terrace
11 Bedroom
12 Ensuite
13 Walk-in wardrobe
14 Bathroom

Ground floor

First floor

Villa Röling

Architectenbureau Paul de Ruiter
Kudelstaart, Netherlands

The inhabitants of Villa Röling are passionate art collectors and wanted their new dwelling to do justice to their collection of paintings and sculptures. The location of their house, at the edge of Lake Westeinderplas, precluded making a closed volume that would limit the view of the surroundings. Therefore the architect decided to design two contrasting volumes: a transparent glass volume overlooking the lake and the garden; and a 'floating' wooden box on top for the works of art.

The ground floor consists of a series of gallery-like spaces offering varying views of the lake and the surroundings. The overall glass façade folds itself almost invisibly around the spaces and creates a contour, which together with the overhanging superstructure, allows for varying incidence of light. On the outside, in front of the glass façade, are cloths that can be pulled up. They not only screen from solar heat, but also create a covered and screened-off terrace.

The wooden box on the upper level contains several large openings. In the centre of the house there is an empty space with a skylight and all four façades contain a large window. At either end of the superstructure are the bedrooms with a maximal view of the surrounding natural environment. Blinds screen from sunlight and solar heat; they are made of horizontal slats and move like shutters. Because they consist of two parts with a bend in the middle, the shutters raise like porches above the glass façade when opened. The paintings and sculptures can be exhibited in the centre of the house around the empty space, allowing natural light to enter both floors.

The overhanging wooden box prevents the sun from warming up the villa by creating shade on the east, west and south side of the villa. Together with the cloths, the heat of the sun can be kept out. The cloths can be operated apart from each other, which makes it possible to adjust the way the cloths are pulled down to the position of the sun. The sustainability and durability of the upper wooden volume is guaranteed by the way the wooden slats are placed. Because the wind can blow through, the wood can dry easily after it has rained.

Water pipes are set in the concrete floors and these cool the concrete floor in summer and heat it in winter. The system is connected by a system of geothermal power – several metres from the villa, pits are placed in the ground from which water with a constant temperature can be extracted and pumped into the villa. The water is cool enough to drink in summer and needs to be heated by a only few degrees in winter, saving a huge amount of energy.

Photography: Pieter Kers

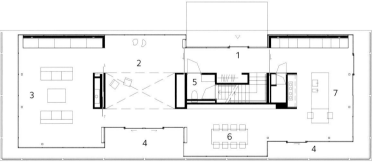

Ground floor

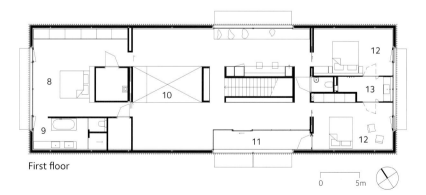

First floor

1 Entry	8 Master bedroom
2 Hall	9 Master ensuite
3 Living room	10 Void
4 Terrace	11 Balcony
5 Water closet	12 Bedroom
6 Dining room	13 Ensuite
7 Terrace	

0   5m

311

villa S | group8
Geneva, Switzerland

Built on cramped lot of land in the heart of a residential neighbourhood, villa S contrasts with the highly traditional villas by which it is surrounded. It is easily recognisable thanks to its front, which forms an S-shape in beige-tinted concrete. This shape brings to mind a cardboard being folded and organises the rooms spatially, while the sand colour brings visual softness to the material. The slabs are linked together by glass, in order to preserve a maximum of transparency and lightness, emphasising the horizontal lines.

The three levels of the house are treated using different materials. By using either raw or coloured building materials, specific ambiance and mood can emerge around the same topic of minimalism.

villa S is brought into relief with clever landscape design – the clean lines and white colour scheme of the deck around the pool highlight its contemporary character.

Photography: dgbp, David Gagnebin-de Bons & Benoît Pointet

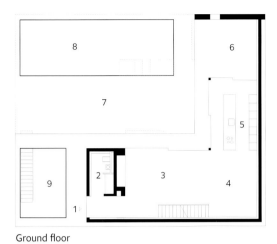

Ground floor

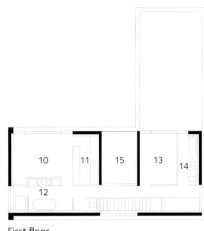

First floor

1 Entry
2 Powder room
3 Living area
4 Dining area
5 Kitchen
6 Covered outdoor dining area
7 Terrace
8 Pool
9 Patio and stair to basement
10 Master bedroom
11 Walk-in wardrobe
12 Master ensuite
13 Bedroom
14 Ensuite
15 Covered terrace

Villa Sow | SAOTA – Stefan Antoni Olmesdahl Truen Architects
Dakar, Senegal

Situated on a cliffside overlooking the Atlantic Ocean, Villa Sow in Dakar, Senegal was designed for a local businessman and his family. Built on the site of an old World War Two bunker, Villa Sow maximises its commanding position to create a house that is not only dramatic but with the incorporation of historical elements quite magical and mysterious. Part of the old bunker has been retained and a portion of it now houses an underground cinema that opens up into a water courtyard/moat that runs along the boundary, creating a water feature at the gateway to the property. It is connected back to the house via a timber-panelled walkway leading to a spiral staircase that runs from the lower ground through to the first floor and second floor levels of the villa.

The ground floor of the house, designed to facilitate seamless indoor and outdoor living and entertainment, is arranged in an L-shape around the pool, the pool terrace and the garden. The formal living and dining spaces cantilever over the cliff and hang over the Atlantic, enjoying panoramic sea views as well as views back to the house. The open kitchen and a separate traditional kitchen, as well as the garage and staff facilities run along the east–west axis and along the northern side of the boundary. From the entrance one moves past the sculptural circular stair to the entertainment room and the double-volume family lounge which connects up with a floating stair to the upper level pyjama lounge, where the bedrooms are located.

One of the features of the house is the spiral staircase, clad in stainless steel, with treads clad in white granite. To add to the sense of continuity between levels, 20mm-diameter stainless steel rods run from the first floor handrail to the lower ground floor, making the stairwell look like a sculptural steel cylinder. A skylight above the stairwell as well as floor-to-ceiling glazing in the lounges add to the sense of transparency. The master bedroom opens on to a large terrace which forms the roof of the more formal living wing of the house and the element which projects over the ocean. The master bathroom opens on to a private garden and outdoor shower situated over the garages. The study sits in a separate block and is joined to the main house by a hallway running along the spine of the building. Under the study is a separate self-contained guest room, alongside a gym and reflecting pond.

The sculptural modernist exterior and shell is counterbalanced by the use of warm and textured materials and finishes. Hardwood timber decks contrast with the textured granite internal floors. Natural timber wall-panels contrasts with the beaten and polished stainless steel panels as well as the black Nero Marquina marble and duco/glass kitchen joinery. Rough-cut quarried stone finishes contrast with smooth marble surfaces. The material selection for the house provided the ideal backdrop for Antoni Associates to make their selection of furniture and decor, from a Carolina Sardi wall installation in the kitchen to their own timber installation in the hallway.

Photography: Stefan Antoni

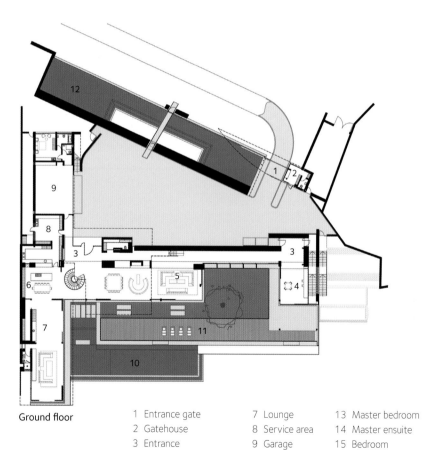

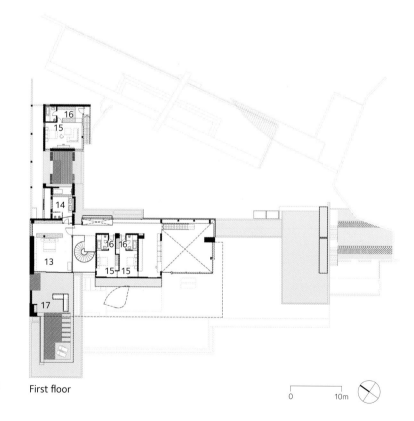

Ground floor

1 Entrance gate	7 Lounge	13 Master bedroom
2 Gatehouse	8 Service area	14 Master ensuite
3 Entrance	9 Garage	15 Bedroom
4 Study	10 Pool	16 Ensuite
5 Lounge	11 Deck	17 Terrace
6 Kitchen/dining area	12 Pond	

First floor

0   10m

Villa Tyto Alba

Norm Applebaum Architect AIA
Escondido, California, USA

A new architecture was born from the ashes of 'Wings', a home designed by architect Norm Applebaum in 1991. The rebirth tells the story of a retired US Ambassador, Richard C. Matheron, his wife Katherine and their architect, Applebaum, based on a friendship which began in the mid-1980s.

The Matherons saw 'Wings' disappear one day in October 2007, taken by a firestorm during the Witch Creek Wildfires. The tragedy occurred in the Escondido area of southern California, above the San Pasqual Valley. The architecture that was lost was featured by Images Publishing in *Another 100 of the World's Best Houses*, published in 2003.

Villa Tyto Alba, the new edifice, sits on a 1-hectare (2.6 acres) plot and was required to be designed with the exact square footage of the previous building – roughly 370 square metres (4000 square feet). Because new challenges had to be fulfilled, the architecture took on a completely different form. The building at the north could no longer cantilever over the slope as the previous home did, and an electrical utility easement on the south side forced the plan to move in different directions within those boundaries.

To design an 'artistically green' architecture was the requirement and because of this the programme possessed the following determinants: geothermal heating, photovoltaic electrical panels, BluWood for framing, recycled blue jeans for wall insulation, foil-faced bubblewrap for roof insulation, bamboo flooring, double-glazing throughout and a 38,000-litre (10,000 gallons) water cistern that captures all of the rainwater from the roof and waters the succulent garden automatically. The house also features decorative leaded windows featuring the barn owl and its natural habitat – a nod to the steel cantilever, a structure made from open-ended rectangular steel fitted for future owl nesting.

Photography: John Durant

Floor plan

1 Entry
2 Master bathroom
3 Master bedroom
4 Master walk-in wardrobe
5 Garage
6 Gallery
7 Kitchen
8 Laundry
9 Verandah
10 Living room
11 Dining room
12 Office
13 Powder room
14 Bedroom
15 Bathroom
16 Reading room

0   4m

Ward Residence

Marmol Radziner
Pacific Palisades, California, USA

Situated in Rustic Canyon, one of the most serene areas in Los Angeles, this new-built 370-square-metre (4000 square feet) residence offers views of the canyon and gently sloping hillsides to the east. The house is effectively divided into two separate but connected areas: a public pavilion including the kitchen, living room and dining areas; and a private pavilion containing the bedrooms. Filtering in the landscape, the site introduces a skewed procession that leads up to the pavilions and looks beyond to the additional structures.

A glass-enclosed walkway forms a bridge between the two masses, taking optimal advantage of the location and surrounding landscape. Created by the inverted design of these two linked pavilions, the orientation of the glass structures peer inward towards the central space. Materials of burnished concrete block, galvanised-steel panelling and glass complement the openness of the design and careful integration of the object-like forms on the site. A double cantilevered guesthouse rests on top of the studio, accentuating the breezeway and intimate arrival space. Working with the landscape in one pictorial image, the simple lap pool lines the back of the property.

Photography: Matthew Millman

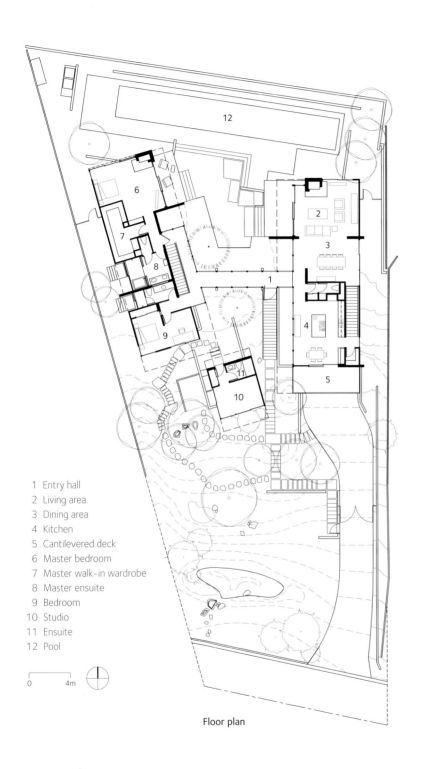

1 Entry hall
2 Living area
3 Dining area
4 Kitchen
5 Cantilevered deck
6 Master bedroom
7 Master walk-in wardrobe
8 Master ensuite
9 Bedroom
10 Studio
11 Ensuite
12 Pool

0   4m

Floor plan

Water Patio

Drozdov & Partners
Odessa, Ukraine

The plot is situated on the edge of a steep plateau and occupies one end in a row of houses. This position invited a creative interpretation of open and closed spaces. One of the aims of this project was to create a harmonious interrelation between the house, the garden and the sea view. These three elements are each placed along the same line and interact in a variety of ways, depending on the position of the observer.

The entire space opens towards the sea. In addition to the outer sea horizon, which is a typical feature of any seaside house, we introduced another water surface – that of the swimming pool, which enhances the visible proximity of the sea. The swimming pool is composed of two parts that can be separated or joined together, depending on the season. The element of water is at the heart of the house, and lends the project its name.

The mirador, with its barbecue spot and sofa, plays an important role in the entire composition. As another strategic point along with the terrace near the swimming pool, it invites a different perception of the house and its environs. Three basic materials were used in the construction of the house: Siberian larch, stucco (resembling Venetian stucco) and copper. The last acquired a noble tint in this coastal environment, which makes it look like rusty steel.

Photography: Andrey Avdeenko

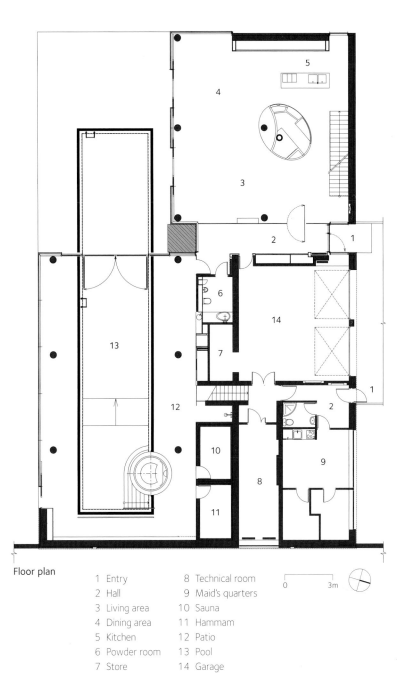

Floor plan

1	Entry	8	Technical room
2	Hall	9	Maid's quarters
3	Living area	10	Sauna
4	Dining area	11	Hammam
5	Kitchen	12	Patio
6	Powder room	13	Pool
7	Store	14	Garage

0   3m

Wenzler Farmhouse | k_m architektur
Langenargen, Germany

This family house was planned and built during the creation of the surrounding agricultural farmstead. The new house is located a short distance from the farm complex, in the middle of an orchard. An elongated one-storey building appears to float slightly above the flat lawn. The flat roof and the north façade, together with a slightly raised floor envelope, are all clad in copper and encase the floor-to-ceiling glazing on the east, west and south façades, in protective fashion.

The large glazed areas and the flat roof make optimal use of solar energy. The large roof overhangs the main core, protecting it from overheating in the summer. A heating pipeline in the farm building, fired with wood from the estate, carry most of the energy for the home. The energy concept is supplemented with a photovoltaic system on the roof of the adjacent farm building and a stove in the living area.

Photography: k_m architektur

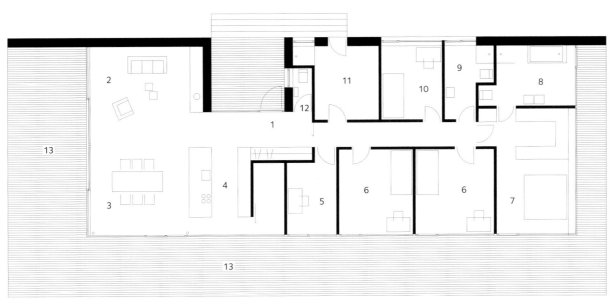

Floor plan

1 Entry
2 Living area
3 Living area
4 Kitchen
5 Office
6 Child's bedroom
7 Master bedroom
8 Master ensuite
9 Bathroom
10 Guest bedroom
11 Laundry/shower room/
  mechanical room
12 Powder room
13 Terrace

Wind-dyed House | acaa
Kanagawa, Japan

This house is located halfway up a cliff, overlooking the ocean. Thick clumps of trees that grow along the slope of the land surrounding the house cast a series of organic silhouettes that make the slope seem to come alive. The architect decided that the appropriate form to build would be as low-lying as possible, while allowing the architecture to become embedded in the surrounding landscape, according to the contours of the terrain. This minimised the effect of the building on the environment. The design of the walls plays an important role in creating the overall projection of the building and prevents the house walls from obstructing or impeding movement and sight.

Glass and screens along the enclosed perimeter of the house give the second floor of the residence a certain transparency. Slender, deep-set eaves cast long shadows on the façade of the building, softening the effect of the building's physical presence in relation to its environment.

The various components of the building were structured in order to allow the inhabitants to enjoy a different view of the outside on each level. The lower ground floor features a stone floor and concrete walls finished with plaster, while the Japanese paper screens fitted inside the glass reflect the shadows of plants and trees. The hard-edged surfaces and finishes co-exist

with the soft, muted tones of the Japanese paper. By contrast, the ground floor features an open-plan living space, the entirety of which can be opened up towards the ocean. A series of wide eaves stand between the outside of the house and the interior, which is articulated into smaller sections by a row of pillars. Going down the staircase-shaped terrace allows one to gradually draw closer to the outdoor landscape. The section that divides the two different elevations on this floor provides seating throughout, functioning as an *engawa* or Japanese-style verandah.

Photography: Hiroshi Ueda

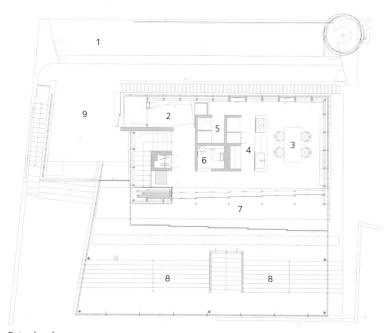

Entry level

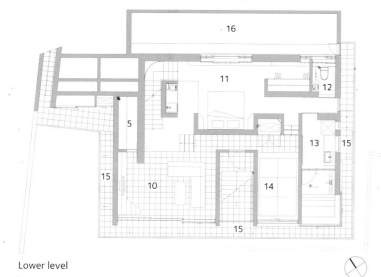

Lower level

1 Approach	9 Garage
2 Entry	10 Living area
3 Dining room	11 Bedroom
4 Kitchen	12 Master water closet
5 Store	13 Ensuite
6 Water closet	14 Tatami room
7 *Engawa* (verandah)	15 Corridor
8 Deck	16 Dry area

Woolamai Hills House

Kerstin Thompson Architects
Cape Woolamai, Victoria, Australia

Taking its cues from agricultural buildings in the surrounding farmland, this home appears to be a prosaic hayshed from afar, yet within its simple skillion form is housed a calm and elegant rural retreat.

The interior is organised by the placement of two plywood sleeping pods under a unifying roof. The first of these pods is the master bedroom suite, which is stepped in plan in response to the topography. The second – which is double storey – accommodates guests and children. The remaining space below the roof is the living area. Sited to enjoy dramatic views to the north and west, the change in ceiling height shifts the feel of this space from domestic and intimate to agrarian and expansive.

The skin of the building is corrugated sheet metal. A substantial portion of this is perforated to provide sun shade and the opportunity for cross-flow ventilation,

while keeping out the flies common to this cattle-filled landscape. A breezeway verandah on the northern side can be used to supplement the living areas and doubles as a sleep-out for hot summer nights. The house can be adjusted according to the seasons – effectively a warm, sunny glasshouse in winter and a cool, shaded breezeway in summer.

In combination with the garage/workshop and above-ground pool, the house works as an ensemble to define a domestic landscape; together they mediate the elements and exposure of this hilltop in the Woolamai range.

Photography: Patrick Bingham-Hall

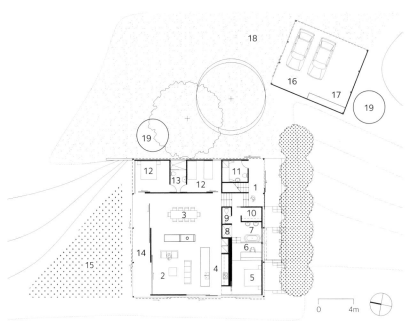

Floor plan

1 Entry	8 Shower	15 Garden
2 Living area	9 Water closet	16 Garage
3 Dining area	10 Walk-in wardrobe	17 Workshop
4 Kitchen	11 Laundry/powder room	18 Guest parking
5 Master bedroom	12 Guest bedroom	19 Water tanks
6 Study	13 Guest ensuite	
7 Master ensuite	14 Verandah	

Yin-Yang House

Brooks + Scarpa
Venice, California, USA

The Yin-Yang House is a single-family home in a quiet neighbourhood in Venice, southern California. The design objective was to create a space for a large and growing family that would create a calm, relaxed and organised environment that emphasises public family space. The home is meant to serve as a place to entertain and a welcoming space for teenagers to seek social space with friends.

The home is organised around a series of courtyards and other outdoor spaces that integrate with the interior of the house. Facing the street the house appears to be solid. However, behind the steel entry door is a courtyard that reveals the indoor–outdoor nature of the house behind the solid exterior. From the entry courtyard, the entire space to the rear garden wall can be seen: the first clue of the home's spatial connection between inside and out. These spaces are designed for entertainment, and the 12-metre (40 feet) sliding glass door to the living room enhances the harmonic relationship with the main room, allowing the owners to host guests without being overburdened.

The tensions of the house's exterior are subtly underscored by a 30-centimetre (12 inch) steel band that hews close to, but sometimes rises above or falls below the floor line of the second floor – a continuous loop moving inside and out like a pen that is never lifted from the page, but reinforces the intention to weave together spatially, as a single space, the indoors with the outside space.

The kitchen is the heart of the house, with an open working area that allows the owner, an accomplished chef, to chat with friends while cooking. Bedrooms are designed to be small and simple to make room for larger public spaces, emphasising the family over individual domains. The breakfast room looks across an outdoor courtyard to the guest room/children's playroom, establishing a visual connection while defining the separation of uses. The children can play outdoors while under adult supervision from inside, or do homework in the office while adults occupy the adjacent outdoor or indoor space.

Many of the materials used, including the bamboo interior, composite stone and tile countertops and bathroom finishes are recycled, and reinforce the environmental credentials of the house, which also has a green roof. Blown-in cellulose insulation, radiant heating and a host of other sustainable features assist in the building's heating and cooling, as do the solar panels, which simultaneously generate power for the house, as well as provide shade.

Photography: John Linden

336

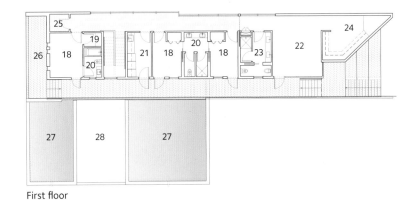

First floor

Ground floor

1 Entry
2 Office
3 Courtyard
4 Living area
5 Dining area
6 Kitchen
7 Pantry
8 Mudroom
9 Garage
10 Covered patio
11 Planter
12 Recreation room
13 Bathroom
14 Shower room
15 Mechanical room
16 Patio
17 Pool
18 Bedroom
19 Walk-in wardrobe
20 Ensuite
21 Laundry
22 Master bedroom
23 Master ensuite
24 Master walk-in wardrobe
25 Storage
26 Front balcony
27 Green roof
28 Open to below

0   4m

Zephyros Villa

Koutsoftides Architects
Pomos, Cyprus

'The shadow of your project is captured in the landscape, so you must first hearken it', said Renzo Piano. From the early stages of the elaboration of sketches for this project, the architect had in mind the words of the great Piano. They wanted to enhance elements that would contribute and reflect these thoughts, so that building and landscape become one, to receive the glorious sun, the western Zephyros wind, the majestic blue sea and the mysterious silver moon; a reminder of when we were children camping and enjoying nature, embracing all the elements under one permanent camping tent.

The house was designed as a holiday house for clients in the UK who eventually decided to leave London to live in Cyprus for good. On approaching the house from the garage driveway, the visitor faces a stone wall and staircase, with the main living area hovering above. The cantilevered mass upstairs provides both shading to the lower ground floor, which accommodates a guest room and an artist's studio, and a sense of playful curiosity, which invites the visitor to the main entrance. The stone for the walls at the lower level was sourced locally from the Pomos region. The decision to use local material enables the lower part of the house to blend seamlessly with the landscape, enhancing the weightlessness of the hovering white box above.

The main entrance to the house is through a Corten steel door, which leads to a second staircase up to the main living areas. On entering there are framed views of the sky, mountains and horizon, with the seascape and Pomos harbour below. Living in Cyprus is a life outdoors, thanks to the weather, so the architect emphasised this by creating a patio with multiple faces, which together with a pool divide the living areas in two. The sliding roofs retract to expose the sky, while the wooden screens, when opened, invite the surrounding landscape to become part of the house.

The house faces north over the small fishing village of Pomos, which was the architect's focal point. The location and the orientation of the property creates a soothing calmness, while the proximity of the cliff and the surrounding fields of lemon, orange and pine trees blend with thyme and other aromatic wild plants. Living in this house means being exposed to the elements, while being protected – as if camping, enjoying every moment of night and day.

Photography: Christos Papantoniou

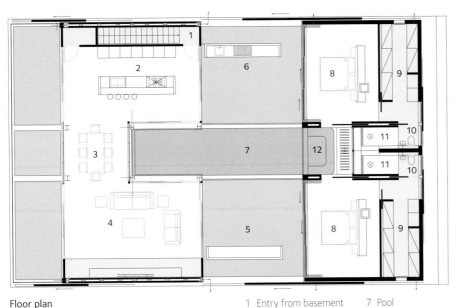

Floor plan

1 Entry from basement
2 Kitchen
3 Dining area
4 Living area
5 Terrace
6 Bar

7 Pool
8 Bedroom
9 Walk-in wardrobe
10 Water closet
11 Ensuite
12 Outdoor shower

Index of Architects

Index of Architects